D0249256

BJ Summers'

POCKET GUIDE TO

Coca-Cola®

Identifications
Current Values
Circa Dates

FIFTH EDITION

COLLECTOR BOOKS
A Division of Schroeder Publishing Co., Inc.

Cover design by Beth Summers
Book layout by Holly C. Long

COLLECTOR BOOKS
P.O. Box 3009
Paducah, Kentucky 42002-3009
www.collectorbooks.com

The current values in this book should be used only as a guide. They are not intended to set prices, which vary from one section of the country to another. Auction prices as well as dealer prices vary greatly and are affected by condition as well as demand. Neither the author nor the publisher assumes responsibility for any losses that might be incurred as a result of consulting this guide.

Searching For A Publisher?

We are always looking for people knowledgeable within their fields. If you feel that there is a real need for a book on your collectible subject and have a large comprehensive collection, contact Collector Books.

Contents

Button sign,
metal, "Yes!
Coke Is Still 5¢,"
1950s,
16" dia., EX,
$775.00 B. *Metz
Superlatives
Auction.*

Dedication

This book is dedicated to thousands in general — and two in particular. To my nephew, Eric Goody Koonzt, a police officer with the Greensboro, North Carolina, police department; and to Brian Kopischke, a relative by marriage who is with the Paducah, Kentucky, police department. To the thousands, unknown to me, who daily risk life and limb safeguarding the freedoms we all take for granted.

Acknowledgments

I would like to extend my sincere thanks to the following people and businesses without whose help this book would have been impossible.

Earlene Mitchell
c/o Collector Books
P.O. Box 3009
Paducah, KY 42002-3009
One of the nicest ladies you'll ever meet. She has been collecting since the 1960s, and is a constant source of information. She remains a very active collector.

Gary Metz's Muddy River Trading Co.
P.O. Box 1430
Salem, VA 24153
Ph. 540-387-5070
Fax 540-387-3233
e-mail: mudauction@aol.com
Gary Metz remains a mainstay in the advertising auction world. Gary's primary emphasis is Coca-Cola, but his auctions always have a broad spectrum of collectible advertising.

Antiques, Cards, and Collectibles
203 Broadway
Paducah, KY 42001
Ph. 270-443-9797
e-mail: ray@haylan.net
Located in historic downtown Paducah, Kentucky, the old Michael Hardware Store is a great place for an afternoon of browsing. Ray Pelley and his friendly staff offer a full line of antiques and collectibles.

Charlie's Antique Mall
303 Main St., P.O. Box 196
Hazel, KY 42049
Ph. 270-492-8175
e-mail: charlies10@aol.com
Located in the historic community of Hazel, Kentucky, on Main Street, this place has it all. The manager, Ray Gough, has some great dealers with a wide variety of antiques and collectibles and some of the friendliest help you'll find. This border-town mall can keep even the pickiest collector busy for the better part of a day.

Farmer's Daughter Antiques
6330 Cairo Rd.
Paducah, KY 42001
Ph. 270-444-7619
This is a neat shop full of primitives and advertising. Easily located one mile west off I-24 at exit 3.

4

Riverbend Auction Company
103 South Monroe St.
P.O. Box 800
Alderson, WV 24910

Patrick's Collectibles
612 Roxanne Dr.
Antioch, TN 37013
Ph. 615-833-4621
If you happen to be around Nashville, Tennessee, during the monthly flea market at the state fairgrounds, be certain to look for Mike and Julie Patrick. They have some of the sharpest advertising pieces you'll ever hope to find. And if Coca-Cola is your field, you won't be able to walk away from the great restored drink machines. Make sure to look them up — you certainly won't be sorry.

Pleasant Hill Antique Mall & Tea Room
315 South Pleasant Hill Rd.
East Peoria, IL 61611
Ph. 309-694-4040
Bob Johnson and the friendly staff at this mall welcome you for a day of shopping. And it'll take that long to work your way through all the quality antiques and collectibles here. When you get tired, stop and enjoy a rest at the tea room, where you can get some of the best home-cooked food found anywhere. All in all, a great place to shop for your favorite antiques.

Creatures of Habit
406 Broadway
Paducah, KY 42001
Ph. 270-442-2923
This business will take you back in time with its wonderful array of vin-tage clothing and advertising. If you a: ever in western Kentucky, stop and s(Natalya and Jack.

The Illinois Antique Center
308 S.W. Commercial
Peoria, IL 61602
Ph. 309-673-3354
This is a day-long stop. Dan ar Kim have restored an old, very larg warehouse overlooking the river i downtown Peoria. It's full of gre. advertising and collectibles. Stop by ar see Dan and Kim and their very frien ly staff, and plan on being amazed.

Rare Bird Antique Mall
212 South Main St.
Goodlettsville, TN 37072
Ph. 615-851-2635
If you find yourself in the great Nashville area, stop by this collectors' pa adise. Jon and Joan Wright have asser bled a great cast of dealers who: offerings run the gamut of collectible me chandise. So step back into a time whe the general store was the place to be, ar be prepared to spend some time.

Riverside Antique Mall
P.O. Box 4425
Sevierville, TN 37864
Ph. 423-429-0100
Located in a new building overloo ing the river, this is a collectors' hea en, full of advertising, with lighte showcases and plenty of friendly hel You need to allow at least half a da for a quick look through this place th sits in the shadows of the Smok Mountains.

Acknowledgments

Bill and Helen Mitchell
226 Arendall St.
Henderson, TN 38340
Ph. 901-989-9302

Bill and Helen have assembled a great variety of advertising with special emphasis on Coca-Cola, and they are always searching for new finds. So if you have anything that fits the bill, give them a call or drop them a letter.

Richard Opfer Auctioneering, Inc.
1919 Greenspring Drive
Timonium, MD 21093
Ph. 410-252-5035

Richard Opfer Auctioneering, Inc., provides a great variey of antiques and collectibles auctions. Give his friendly staff a call for his next auction catalog.

Wm. Morford
RD #2
Cazenovia, NY 13035
Ph. 315-662-7625

Wm. Morford has been operating one of the country's better cataloged phone auction businesses for several years. He doesn't list reproductions or repairs that are deceptive in nature. Each catalog usually has a section with items that are for immediate sale. Try out this site and tell him where you got his name and address.

Also thanks to Joe Wilson, Brian and Christy Kopischke, and Charles Fletcher.

If I have omitted anyone who should be here, please be assured it is an oversight on my part and is not intentional.

Poster, cardboard, "Welcome Friend," lettering on background designed to resemble simulated oak, 1957, 14" x 12", EX, $375.00 C.
Mitchell Collection.

COCA-COLA!!! Just the magic name will bring a smile to the lips and memories of good times. These memories are different for each of us. One might be the family dinner on Christmas Eve — nothing better than Kentucky Bar-B-Que, chips, fresh moist coconut cake, and of course, ice-cold Coca-Cola. Maybe one is of the ballpark on a clear summer day, with a light breeze and a stadium vendor with cold Coke. One of my favorite memories involves a large shade tree in the country at the grandparents, surrounded by family, with ice-cold Coke and peanuts in the small hobbleskirt bottle. And when finished there was always a bet on the city.

Coke is now loved and recognized all over the world. In all of America's good times, Coke has been a steady product, like a big brother. During time of turmoil, Coke has been a pillar of strength. During World War II, Coke established bottling plants overseas to supply American GIs with the familiar hometown drink. And in an effort to help bolster the folks at home, advertising was geared toward a feeling of peaceful better times. Kids the world over regularly leave a cold bottle of Coke for Santa. With the image of Coke Santa in mind, of course, as provided by artist Haddom Sundblom. Coke needs no introduction. It's as American as both Mom's apple pie and baseball.

To become an American icon and hold the lion's share of the market for so many years is no small feat. So much of Coke's fame is due to advertising. *Fantastic, colorful, wholesome, memory provoking,* and of course *plentiful* are just a few of the words and phrases that describe Coca-Cola advertising. For us collectors, to be at a Coke swap meet is to be like a kid in a toy store at Christmas.

This book is meant only as a *guid* and not as the last word on values. It another tool in the collector's arsenal information; remember, an informe collector is the one who is smiling the end of the day.

I've attempted to help both th advanced and beginning collector wit this book. I don't attempt to set prices c any Coke memorabilia, only to repo values. *These values are meant to l only a guide, not absolute.* If you're bu ing, you will no doubt like that sentenc But if you're selling, it won't be ; appealing. When you look at the captio you will see that I have keyed the pric so that you'll know the origin of th value. You'll see the following key syr bols throughout this book:

C — a value given to me by a collector(s)

B — a value determined by an auction price (Remember on auction values that two determined bidders can run a price far past fair market value. Likewise, lack of interest will sometimes let a collectible sell for less than it should.)

D — a value determined by a dealer

Condition will be graded by the fc lowing key:

NOS — refers to new old stock, usually found in a warehouse or store closed for some time

NRFB — never removed from box

MIB — absolutely mint, still in the original container

M — mint condition; however, has been out of the container

NM — near mint, nothing to detract from display

EX — excellent; very minor distractions, such as shelf wear, don't detract from the focal point

VG — very good, may have light scratches on the edges or back, but nothing to detract from the face

G — good, the usual used condition, with scratches and nicks on the item front, but still desirable

F — fair, some bad detractions

P — poor; pick it up only because of its rarity or because it is a piece you don't have in your collection.

Of course other factors, such as location, will affect price. Generally speaking, an item with a $100.00 price in my area (the Midwest and the South) may sell in the $150.00 – 175.00 range on the East Coast and in the Northeast, and in the $200.00 – 225.00 range on the West Coast.

How tough is the demand in my area? I'm a long-time collector of items from my hometown of Paducah, Ken-tucky. Fortunately for me, the city has a very colorful and rich history, with some great memorabilia. Unfortunately for me, there are several die-hard collectors like myself, and among us, we keep the prices artificially high due to the demand for those few items that are always surfacing.

Probably the most important consideration of pricing is condition. This is where I find the most problems. If an item in the price guide is labeled as mint at $200.00, and you see one in a store in fair condition at $200.00, it's overpriced. Don't buy it! I've attempted to make sure all of the listings in this book have the condition listed. This should help when it's time to buy or haggle. It's extremely difficult to find a seller and a buyer that agree on an item's value. A buyer shouldn't be hesitant about making an offer, and a seller shouldn't be offended by an offer. Good luck buying, selling, and collecting.

Wall-hung sign, wood and metal, "Drink Coca-Cola" button at bottom, slide menu strips, 1940s, EX, $65.00 B. *Metz Superlatives Auction.*

Aluminum, die-cut script, "Drink Coca-Cola in Bottles," designed for truck radiator, 1920s, 17½" x 7½", EX, $375.00 B. *Metz Superlatives Auction.*

Banner, canvas, "Drink Coca-Cola from the Bottle through a Straw," with straight-sided bottle at left, 1910, 70" x 16", EX, $4,000.00 B. *Metz Superlatives Auction.*

Banner, canvas, "Coca-Cola brings you Edgar Bergen with Charlie McCarthy..." truck mounted, 1950s, 60" x 42", EX, $1,100.00 B. *Metz Superlatives Auction.*

Base, cast iron, "Drink Coca-Cola." There are a lot of reproductions of this — most have a different measurement and the lettering is different, so be careful. 21" dia., VG, $195.00 C.

Baseball score-
board, cardboard,
very heavy stock,
advertising panel
at top ,
"Drink...in Bot-
tles 5¢," unusual
item and still
with good colors,
1930s,
30" x 20", EX,
$1,000.00 B. *Metz
Superlatives
Auction.*

Bottle, cardboard,
hobbleskirt bottle
with no message,
Canadian, 13" x 33",
EX, $475.00 B. *Metz
Superlatives Auction.*

Bottle, celluloid,
"Drink ...Delicious
and Refreshing,"
straight-sided bottle
with paper label,
1900s,
6" x 13", VG,
$2,600.00 B.

Bottle, cardboard, with
courtesy panel for
pricing, NOS, new,
14" x 45", NM, $10.00 C.

Bottle, metal, "Coca-Cola...Sign of Good Taste," self
framing with fishtail logo and hobbleskirt bottle, 1960s,
31¼" x 11¼", G, $295.00 C.

Bottle, metal, "Drink Coca-Cola," flat mount, horizontal, featuring tilted
hobbleskirt bottle in yellow spotlight, 1948, 54" x 18", VG, $395.00 C.

Bottle, metal, "Drink Coca-
Cola...Sold Here Ice Cold,"
flat mount, vertical, self
framing with Christmas
bottle in center, 1932, EX,
$695.00 D. *Rivervside
Antique Mall.*

Bottle, metal, "Drink Coca-Cola," self framing with hobbleskirt bottle to right of message, 1950s, 54" x 18", EX, $450.00 C. *Eric Reinfield.*

Bottle, metal, flat mount, die cut, embossed, 36" tall, G, $350.00 B. *Metz Superlatives Auction.*

Bottle, metal, "Have a Coke...Coca-Cola," flat mount, vertical, bottle in center yellow spotlight, 1940s, 18" x 54", EX, $395.00 C.

Bottlers' advance calendar print, paper, "Two Ladies at the Beach," extremely rare piece, framed under glass, 1917, NM, $8,500.00 C. *Mitchell Collection.*

Bottle topper, cardboard, die-cut pretty redheaded girl with tray, when placed over the neck of a bottle gives a 3-D effect, 1920s, 11½" x 14", NM, $2,600.00 B. *Metz Superlatives Auction.*

Bottle topper, cardboard, for "King Size Ice Cold," also has string for use as a hanger or pull, 1960s, $100.00 – 175.00 C. *Joe Wilson.*

Bottle topper, cardboard, six-pack and food in basket, top hole fits over bottle neck, 1950s, 8" x 7", NM, $550.00 B.

Bottle topper, paper, "Regular Size Coca-Cola" with Santa's elves looking around the carton, 9" x 11¾", EX, $45.00 – 55.00 C.

Bottle topper, plastic, designed to sit on top of a hobbleskirt bottle, "We Let You See the Bottle," 1950s, EX, $495.00 – 550.00 C. *Mitchell Collection.*

Bumper sticker, vinyl, with Max Headroom "Don't Say The 'P' Word," 1980s, EX, $15.00 C.

Cash register topper, metal and plastic, "Drink Coca-Cola," 1950s, EX, $950.00 B. *Metz Superlatives Auction.*

Counter top, metal, "Lunch with Us..." light-up by Price Brothers, 1950s, 19" x 8½", EX, $900.00 B. *Metz Superlatives Auction.*

Crossing guard, metal and cast iron, "Slow School Zone." *Note: these have been reproduced. Usually the details and thickness of the metal give away the fakes; also watch for fake bases — they aren't the same diameter of the originals and the lettering isn't the same.* Pricing is still volatile, ranging between $1,000.00 and $3,500.00 depending upon condition and how it is sold, whether auction, dealer, etc., 1950s.

Decal, vinyl, "Drink Coca-Cola...Please Pay Cashier," 1960s, EX, $30.00 C.

Display, cardboard, "Boy-oh Boy!" 3-D set-up of boy in front of store cooler with a bottle of Coke, 1937, 36" x 34", VG, $925.00 C. *Mitchell Collection.*

Display, cardboard, "Buy the Case Coke...10 oz. Size," "$1.25 Plus Deposit," EX, $65.00 – 95.00 C.

Display, cardboard, "Coca-Cola...Ice Cold," die cut with diamond can in hand, 1960s, NM, $230.00 B. *Metz Superlatives Auction.*

Display, cardboard, "Coca-Cola...Ice Cold," featuring a king- size bottle die cut, 1960s, NM, $160.00 B. *Metz Superlatives Auction.*

Display, cardboard, "Coca-Cola...Dale Earnhardt" die-cut life-size standup. Prices shot up to around $100.00 – 125.00 immediately after his death; before that, they had been in the $10.00 – 15.00 range. They have started a very slow decline. NM, $85.00 C.

Display, cardboard, die-cut bottle in hand beside sign, on post that reads "Drink...Delicious and Refreshing," 1900s, 9" x 19", F, $525.00 C.

Display, cardboard, die-cut boy and
girl drinking Coke from a glass
through a straw, button in front and
"So Refreshing," 1950s, 20" x 13", VG,
$195.00 C. *Metz Superlatives Auction.*

Display, cardboard, die-cut
"Old Man North" with a car-
ton of Cokes, "Serve Ice
Cold," 1953, 16" x 21", NM,
$275.00 B. *Metz Superlatives
Auction.*

Display, cardboard, die-cut
boy with dog, sitting on
stump and fishing, bottle of
Coke in one hand, "Friends
for Life," unusual piece, not
seen very often, 1935, 36"
tall, VG, $2,650.00 B. *Metz
Superlatives Auction.*

Display, cardboard, die cut of woman holding a six-pack carton, 1940s, 5' tall, EX, $275.00 C. *Metz Superlatives Auction.*

Display, cardboard, die-cut unit for "Beverage Dept." with a "Drink" button at top, 1954, 26" x 36", EX, $700.00 B. *Metz Superlatives Auction.*

Display, cardboard, die-cut winter girl with glasses of Coke in snow, 1930 – 1940s, 32" x 19", EX, $695.00 C.

Display, card- board, "Drink Coca-Cola," die- cut sundial with couple under a parasol, 1911, 36" x 29", EX, $4,000.00 B. *Metz Superlatives Auction.*

Display, cardboard, "Drink Coca-Cola," die- cut easel- back boy at soda fountain with glass of Coke and a sandwich, 1936, 28" x 36", EX, $2,800.00 B. *Metz Superlatives Auction.*

Display, cardboard, "Drive with Real Refreshment," bottle cap coming off with product emerging, 1999, 8" x 8", NM, $15.00 D.

Display, cardboard, "Enjoy a Float with COKE," with a courtesy panel for "Today's Feature," 22" x 7", NM, $65.00 C. *Mitchell Collection.*

Display, cardboard, "Float with Coke," string hung, resembles a life ring, 1960s, 10" dia., EX, $95.00 C.

Display, cardboard, "For Extra Fun...Take More Than One," life-size cut-out of Jennifer O'Neill with a six-pack carton in each hand, 1960s, 60" x 30", EX, $130.00 B. *Metz Superlatives Auction.*

Display, cardboard, "Off to a Fresh Start," diecut woman wearing a smile and 1920 to 1930s vintage clothing, 1931, 12" x 27", EX, $875.00 B. *Metz Superlatives Auction.*

Display, cardboard, rack sign, die-cut Eddie Fisher, 1954, 12" x 20", EX, $175.00 C.

Display, cardboard and plastic, "Work Safely," light-up with three work figures carrying a banner that reads, "Work Safety-wise," 1950s, 15½" sq., EX, $725.00 B. *Metz Superlatives Auction.*

Display, cardboard, ringmaster and assistant die-cut pieces, matted and framed under glass, 1920 – 1930s, 32" tall, EX, $550.00 C. *Metz Superlatives Auction.*

Display, cardboard, "Take Enough Home...2 Convenient Sizes," 1956, 29" x 32", EX, $525.00 B. *Metz Superlatives Auction.*

Display, cardboard, two-piece with two couples having a picnic, "Buy Coca-Cola Now...for Picnic Fun," 1950s, EX, $135.00 – 185.00 C. *Mitchell Collection.*

Display, celluloid, "Drink Coca-Cola High-balls," 1921, 11¼" x 6", EX, $6,500.00 D. *Metz Superlatives Auction.*

Display, cardboard, window cutout from Niagara Litho Co., NY, with woman in front of cooler holding a bottle of Coke, 1940s, 32½" x 42½", EX, $975.00 – 1,400.00 C. *Mitchell Collection.*

Display, glass and plastic, "Always Feels Right, Always Coca-Cola," light-up counter display with newer plastic bottle, 1990s, 12" x 13", NM, $250.00 B. *Metz Superlatives Auction.*

Display, glass mirror, "Drink Carbonated Coca-Cola 5¢ in bottles," round, G, $600.00 C. *Mitchell Collection.*

Display, metal, "Curb Service...Coca-Cola...Sold
Here Ice Cold," embossed
lettering, driveway sign,
1931, 20" x 28", EX,
$125.00 B. *Metz Superlatives
Auction.*

Display, metal, "Drink
Coca-Cola...Fountain Ser-
vice," double-sided shield,
1934, 23" x 26", NM,
$1,600.00 C.

Display, metal, "Drink Coca-Cola...Ice Cold,"
horizontal, tag design with bottle, 1950s, EX,
$700.00 B. *Metz Superlatives Auction.*

Display, metal, "Enjoy Coca-
Cola...While We Check Your
Tires," 1960s, EX, $3,400.00 C.

Display, metal, "Drink Coca-Cola in Bottles," on metal surrounded by bent wire frame, 1950s, EX, $300.00 B. *Metz Superlatives Auction.*

Display, metal, "Gas Today...Drink Coca-Cola While You Wait," with courtesy panel for gas prices, 1929 – 1930, 28" x 20", EX, $4,500.00 B. *Metz Superlatives Auction.*

Display, metal, "Ice Cold...Coca-Cola...Enjoy That Refreshing New Feeling," horizontal, fishtail logo with bottle, 1960s, EX, $525.00 B. *Metz Superlatives Auction.*

Display, glass and plastic, "Drink Coca-Cola...Pause and Refresh" on left side and fan image of bottle in hand on right side, 1940s, 19" x 15½", EX, $675.00 B. *Metz Superlatives Auction.*

Display, metal and glass, "Please Pay When Served," light-up counter sign, 1948, 20" x 12", VG, $2,000.00 C. *Metz Superlatives Auction.*

Display, metal and glass, "Drink ...in Bottles," disc-shaped motion light, 1950, 11½" dia., NM, $675.00 B. *Metz Superlatives Auction.*

Display, metal and glass, "Have a Coke...Refresh Yourself," light-up arrow pointing at cup, difficult to locate, 1950s, 17" x 10" x 3", NM, $1,400.00 B. *Metz Superlatives Auction.*

Display, metal and plastic, "Drink
Coca-Cola," light-up with starburst
effect in back of cup, 1960s,
14" x 16", EX, $575.00 C.
Collectors Auction Services.

Display, metal and plastic, "Drink
Coca-Cola in Bottles...Shop
Refreshed...Take Enough Home,"
light-up with rotating top, 1950s, 21"
tall, EX, $525.00 B.

Display, metal and plas-
tic, "Have a Coke" with
bottle in hand, light-up
with beveled edge,
1940s, 18" x 12", EX,
$775.00 B. *Metz Superla-
tives Auction.*

Display, neon and metal, "Drink
Coca-Cola in Bottles," with the original crinkle paint, super early piece,
influenced by the Art Deco era and
difficult to find. *Caution: this item
has been reproduced; however, the
reproduction is very easy to detect.*
1939, 17" x 13½", G, $1,700.00 B.
Metz Superlatives Auction.

Display, neon and metal, "Coca-Cola in
Bottles," Art Deco–influenced base, rubber feet for
counter use, 1950s, EX, $3,000.00 B.
Metz Superlatives Auction.

Display, paper, "Drink Coca-Cola...See
Kit Carson TV Show..." featuring Kit Car-
son, 1953, 24" x 16", EX, $145.00 C.
Mitchell Collection.

Display, wood and plastic, "Drink
Coca-Cola..." fishtail design over
courtesy panel, 1960s, 15½" x 12",
VG, $145.00 C.

Display; wood, glass, and chrome; "Coca-
Cola...Please Pay when Served," cash register
topper, 1940s, 11½" x 6", EX, $900.00 B. *Metz
Superlatives Auction.*

Display, wood and metal, "Drink Coca-Cola...Ice Cold" on disc with bottle and arrow, 1939, 17" dia., G, $450.00 C.

Driveway, metal,"Drink Coca-Cola Refresh," lollipop sign with correct base, 1940 – 1950s, F, $595.00 D.

Flange, metal, "Drink Coca-Cola...Enjoy That Refreshing New Feeling," center fishtail logo, 1960s, 18" x 15", VG, $350.00 C.

Flange, metal, "Drink Coca-Cola...Ice Cold," die cut with button top and arrow flange arm, hobbleskirt bottle, EX, $575.00 D.

Flange, metal, "Drink Coca-Cola...Soda," button on top, 1950s, EX, $3,300.00 B. *Metz Superlatives Auction.*

Flange, metal, "Sign of Good Taste," double sided with fishtail logo in center, green stripes, NOS, 1960s, 17¾" x 15", NM, $300.00 B. *Wm. Morford Investment Grade Collectibles.*

Flange, porcelain, "Coca-Cola Iced Here," 18" x 20", EX, $775.00 C.

Flat mount, metal, "Coca-Cola...at Home...Handy Home Carton Sold Here...Now Enjoy," cardboard six-pack, Canadian, hard to find, 1930s, 18" x 54", F, $1,050.00 B. *Metz Superlatives Auction.*

Flat mount, glass, "Drink Coca-Cola," reverse-painted glass, 1920s, 10" x 6", EX, $1,350.00 C.

Flat mount, metal, "Coca-Cola...Delicious and Refreshing," oval self framing, Lillian Nordica beside table, rare item, 1904, 8½" x 10¼", EX, $8,500.00 D.

Flat mount, metal, "Coca-Cola...Delicious and Refreshing...Take a Case Home Today," painted, 19½" x 27¾", VG, $250.00 D.

Flat mount, metal, "Coca-Cola," self framing with fishtail logo, diamond can on right and bottle on left, 1960s, 54" x 18", NM, $850.00 B. *Metz Superlatives Auction.*

Flat mount, metal, "Coca-Cola...Sign of Good Taste," fishtail design on striped frame, 1960s, 46" x 16", EX, $325.00 C.

Flat mount, metal, die-cut embossed six-pack
with "King Size" panel at bottom, 1963, 36" x
30", EX, $700.00 B.
Metz Superlatives Auction.

Flat mount, metal, "Drink Coca-Cola," couple with bottle of
Coke, self framing, 1940s, 35" x 11", EX, $595.00 D.

Flat mount, metal,
"Drink Coca-
Cola...Ice Cold
5¢," vertical design
with hobbleshirt
bottle, 1936, EX,
$2,700.00 B. *Metz
Superlatives Auction.*

Flat mount, metal, "Drink Coca-Cola...Ice Cold,"
embossed with shadowed 1923 bottle to left of message panel, 1936, 28" x 20", EX, $850.00 B. *Metz
Superlatives Auction.*

Flat mount, metal, "Drink Coca-Cola in Bottles"embossed
painted kick plate with bottle in left of message panel, 1931,
27" x 10", EX, $750.00 B. *Metz Superlatives Auction.*

Flat mount, metal, "Drink Coca-Cola...Lunches and Home
Made Chili...," green striped background with rolled edges,
1960 – 1970s, 65" x 35", EX, $235.00 C.

Flat mount, metal, "Drink Coca-Cola," self framing, designed for outdoor use, with courtesy panel at top, 1950 – 1960s, 72" x 36", F, $95.00 B. *Metz Superlatives Auction.*

Flat mount, metal, "Drink Coca-Cola...Take Home a Carton" vertical design with six for 25¢ carton in yellow spotlight in sign center, Canadian made, 1942, 17" x 53½", EX, $825.00 C.

Flat mount, metal, "Drink Coca-Cola...Sign of Good Taste," vertical fishtail over bottle, 1960s, 18" x 54", EX, $350.00 B. *Metz Superlatives Auction.*

Flat mount, metal, "Drink Coca-Cola," unusual "marching" bottles, 1937, 54" x 18", NM, $800.00 B. *Metz Superlatives Auction.*

Flat mount, metal, "Enjoy Big King Size...Coca-Cola...Ice Cold," self framing, fishtail logo with bottle, 1960s, 56" x 32", EX, $375.00 B.

Flat mount, metal, "Luncheonette...Coca-Cola," with fishtail logo and bottle and diamond can, 59¼" x 23¼", EX, $425.00 C.

Flat mount, metal, "Pause...Drink Coca-Cola," self framing with horizontal detail. This one is considered rare due to the 1939 – 1940 cooler in yellow spotlight, 1940, 42" x 18", EX, $2,400.00 B. *Metz Superlatives Auction.*

Flat mount, metal, "Pickup 6...for Home Refreshment," with six-pack carton pictured, self framing with rolled edges, 1956, 50" x 16", NM, $1,450.00 B.

Flat mount, metal, "Pickup 12...Refreshment for All," 12-pack of bottles in center, self-framing rolled edges, 1960s, 50" x 16", EX, $595.00 C.

Flat mount, metal, "Taste TAB...Flavor In — Calories Out...a Product of the Coca-Cola Company," self framing with rolled edges, 1960s, 31½" x 12", VG, $275.00 C.

Flat mount, paper, "Drink Coca-Cola...Coca-Cola Brings You Edgar Bergen with Charlie McCarthy...CBS Sunday Evenings," Edgar and Charlie in front of an old CBD microphone, 1949, 22" x 11", EX, $250.00 C. *Mitchell Collection.*

Flat mount, paper, "Drink Coca-Cola, Quick Refreshment," with hobbleskirt bottle and hot dog, framed, EX, $195.00 C. *Mitchell Collection.*

Flat mount, paper, pretty girl with large red bow on white dress drinking from a straight-sided bottle with a straw, matted, framed and under glass, 1910s, F, $3,950.00 C. *Mitchell Collection.*

Flat mount, paper, "Tome Coca-Cola" with swimming star Lupe Velez holding up a bottle of Coke, 1932, 11" x 21½", NM, $1,250.00 C. *Mitchell Collection.*

Flat mount, porcelain, "Buvez Coca-Cola Vendu Ici Glace," French, single sided, 30½" x 12", EX, $225.00 C.

Flat mount, porcelain, "Coca-Cola...Sold Here Ice Cold," 1940s, 29" x 12", EX, $325.00 C.

Flat mount, porcelain, "Drink Coca-Cola...Fountain Service," Canadian, 1935, 27" x 14", NM, $1,425.00 D. *Metz Superlatives Auction.*

Flat mount, porcelain, "Delicious Refreshing" with hobbleskirt in center, 1950s, 24" sq., EX, $325.00 C. *Metz Superlatives Auction.*

Flat mount, porcelain, "Drink Coca-Cola," with rolled ends, 1950s, 44" x 16", M, $325.00 B.

Hanging, glass, "Please Pay when Served...Coca-Cola," reverse glass, 1950s, 19" x 9½", EX, $550.00 B. *Metz Superlatives Auction.*

Hanging, metal, "Drink Coca-Cola," Kay Displays, 1940s, F, $80.00 B. *Metz Superlatives Auction.*

Hanging, metal, "Coca-Cola...Sold Here...Ice Cold," die cut, double sided, arrow shaped. *Caution: This sign has been heavily reproduced.* 1927, 30" x 8", VG, $450.00 D.

Hanging, metal, "Rx Drug Rx...Coca-Cola...Store," designed to hang on arm over sidewalk, EX, $1,300.00 C.

Hanging, metal, "Savourez Coca-Cola À La Maison," French Canadian, 1930-40s, 11" x 16", EX, $200.00 B. *Metz Superlatives Auction.*

Hanging, porcelain, "Drink Coca-Cola," double sided, 52½" x 35½", F, $150.00 C.

Hanging, porcelain, "Drink Coca-Cola," double sided, add-on bottle disc on bottom adds a 3-D effect, 1923, 48" x 60", G, $675.00 C.

Kay Displays, plywood, "Drink Coca-Cola" with applied wood war ships, complete set of five, 1940s, 25" x 8½", EX, $1,900.00 B. *Metz Superlatives Auction.*

Kay Displays, wood and brass, "Drink Coca-Cola," shield shaped with die-cut filigree at top, 1940s, 19" x 20", G, $800.00 B. *Metz Superlatives Auction.*

Kay Displays, wood, "Drink Coca-Cola...Ice Cold," arrow pointing down through triangle with bottle in point of arrow, 1940s, 24" x 28", G, $750.00 B. *Metz Superlatives Auction.*

Kay Displays, wood, "Here's Refreshment" with bottle and horseshoe on plank, 1940s, 16½" x 12", VG, $395.00 C.

PAUSE . HERE .

DRINK
Coca-Cola

Kay Displays, wood and metal, "Drink Coca-Cola...Pause Here,"
1930s, 37" x 10", G, $1,625.00 D.

Pilaster, metal, "Drink
Coca-Cola in Bottles...Pick-
up 12...Refreshment for
All," with 16" button at top
and 12-pack carton, 1954,
16" x 55", NM, $3,300.00 B.
Metz Superlatives Auction.

Pilaster, metal, "Drink
Coca-Cola...Refresh
Yourself," unusual ver-
sion with the "Refresh"
top tag, 1950s, 16" x 52",
EX, $1,400.00 B. *Metz
Superlatives Auction.*

Pilaster, metal, "Drink
Coca-Cola...Serve Coke
at Home," 16" button at
top with 6-pack carton,
1948, 16" x 54", NM,
$700.00 D.

41

Poster, cardboard, "12 Bottle Carton...More for Everybody," framed and under glass, 1950s, 16" x 27", VG, $155.00 B. *Metz Superlatives Auction.*

Pilaster, metal, "Take Home a Carton of Quality Refreshment," with a cardboard six-pack carton at the bottom, 1950s, 16" x 55", NM, $875.00 B. *Wm. Morford Investment Grade Collectibles.*

Poster, cardboard, "All Set at Our House" with young redheaded boy holding a six-pack of Cokes, 1943, EX, $650.00 B.

Poster, cardboard, "At Home," vertical scene of friends and a bowl of iced Cokes, 1953, 16" x 27", VG, $475.00 B. *Metz Superlatives Auction.*

Poster, cardboard, "Be Really Refreshed," die-cut double-sided pretty woman with a glass of Coke, 1960s, 13" x 17", EX, $425.00 B. *Metz Superlatives Auction.*

Poster, cardboard, "Coca-Cola Belongs," military couple at booth, 1930s, 36" x 20", EX, $1,100.00 B. *Metz Superlatives Auction.*

Poster, cardboard, "Coca-Cola 5¢," woman with broad-brimmed hat seated with bamboo fan, 1912, EX, $4,900.00 D.

Poster, cardboard, "Coca-Cola," Chinese girl seated with a glass of Coke, 1936, 14½" x 22", NM, $1,450.00 C.

Poster, cardboard, "Coca-Cola Refresh-
ing" young lady enjoying a bottle of
Coke, in original wooden frame, 1949,
G, $375.00 B. *Metz Superlatives Auction.*

Poster, cardboard, "Coca-
Cola" vertical, woman with
small kitten and ball of
twine being offered a Coke,
foreign, 1950s, 16" x 27",
EX, $250.00 B. *Metz
Superlatives Auction.*

Poster, cardboard, "Coke," double-sided vertical dis-
play with Old Man North on one side and bottles of
Coke being passed around on the other side, French
Canadian, 16" x 27", VG, $225.00 C. *Metz Superlatives
Auction.*

Poster, cardboard, "Coke Head-quarters" with a young couple at the refrigerator with Coke, 1947, EX, $455.00 D.

Poster, cardboard, "Coke Time," pretty woman in cowboy hat, bottle of Coke, border is surrounded by various cattle brands, 1955, VG, $375.00 C.

Poster, cardboard, "Coke Knows No Season," couple in background waving, Coke bottle in snow bank, with original wooden frame, 1946, 62" x 33", G, $450.00 C.

Poster, cardboard, "Drink Coca-Cola...Be Alert," soda jerk with extended glass of Coke, easel back for counter use, unusual piece, 1930s, 21" x 37", EX, $4,300.00 B. *Metz Superlatives Auction.*

Poster, cardboard, "Coke Time," two couples enjoying themselves with Coke, in original restored frame, 1954, NM, $600.00 B. *Metz Superlatives Auction.*

Poster, cardboard, "Demand the Genuine by Full Name, Nicknames Encourage Substitution" with straight-sided paper-label bottle, 1914, 30" x 18", F, $500.00 B. *Metz Superlatives Auction.*

Poster, cardboard, "Drink Coca-Cola...Delicious and Refreshing...Refreshment You Go For," horizontal with girl on bicycle with front basket full of Cokes, 36" x 20", NM, $675.00 B. *Metz Superlatives Auction.*

Poster, cardboard, "Drink Coca-Cola...Come up Smiling" with Johnny Weissmuller and Maureen O'Sullivan sitting on a springboard, 1934, 13½" x 29½", EX, $3,100.00 C. *Mitchell Collection.*

Poster, cardboard, "Drink Coca-Cola," Hostess Girl sitting on the arm of chair and enjoying a bottle of Coke, 1935, 16" x 27", F, $250.00 D.

Poster, cardboard, "Drink Coca-Cola...Delicious with Good Food," woman with serving tray full of food and Cokes, Canadian, 1931 – 1932, 18" x 32", EX, $4,100.00 B. *Metz Superlatives Auction.*

Poster, cardboard, "Drink Coca-Cola ...Refresh Yourself," horizontal, three cheerleaders with Cokes, 1953, 27" x 16", EX, $675.00 B. *Metz Superlatives Auction.*

Poster, cardboard, "Drink Coca-Cola," pretty dark-haired lady with a horse and a bottle, 1938, 30" x 50", G, $1,050.00 D.

Poster, cardboard, "Drink Coca-
Cola...Refreshing," vertical running girl as used on the 1937
tray, 1937, 14" x 30", EX,
$400.00 C.

Poster, cardboard, "Enjoy That
Refreshing New Feeling," couple at
waters edge with refreshing Coke
in bottles, 1960s, 19" x 27", EX,
$175.00 C.

Poster, cardboard, "Entertain Your
Thirst...the One Drink Most Guests
Prefer," 1956, 16" x 15", EX,
$130.00 B. *Metz Superlatives Auction.*

Poster, cardboard, "Face Your Job Refreshed," pretty woman in work environment at drill press, 1940s, 59" x 30", VG, $900.00 D.

Poster, cardboard, "-et Coke, Aussi," French Canadian with mother and daughter at table with bottles of Coke, 1946, 16" x 27", VG, $275.00 C.
Metz Superlatives Auction.

Poster, cardboard, "Face the Sun Refreshed," young woman using one hand to shield eyes from the sun and holding a bottle of Coke with the other hand, vertical display, 1941, 30" x 53½", VG, $675.00 C.

Poster, cardboard, "Extra Bright Refreshment," couple at party holding bottles of Coke, 33" x 53", EX, $325.00 C.

Poster, cardboard, "For People on the Go," vertical, serviceman and pretty lady walking with a bottle of Coke, 1944, 28" x 36", EX, $1,300.00 B. *Metz Superlatives Auction.*

Poster, cardboard, "For the Party," soldier and pretty girl on bicycle for two with a basket full of Coke bottles, 1940s, 29" x 50½", EX, $525.00 C.

Poster, cardboard, "Good Taste," 50s girl and furniture, 1955, 16" x 27", EX, $625.00 B. *Metz Superlatives Auction.*

Poster, cardboard, "Good Taste for All," bottle in hand, 1955, 16" x 27", EX, $295.00 C.

Poster, cardboard, "Got Enough Coke on Ice?" three teenage girls on sofa with telephone, Canadian, 1945, 36" x 20", G, $400.00 C.

Poster, cardboard, "Have a Coke...Coca-Cola," couple at a masquerade ball, F, $275.00 C.

Poster, cardboard, "Have a Coke" pretty girl pulling on skates, 1955, F, $500.00 B. *Metz Superlatives Auction*.

Poster, cardboard, "Here's Something good!" party scene with people enjoying a Coke, 1951, EX, $375.00 C. *Metz Superlatives Auction.*

Poster, cardboard, "Hello Refreshment," vertical version, pretty girl coming out of swiming pool, 1942, EX, $600.00 B. *Metz Superlatives Auction.*

Poster, cardboard, "Home Refreshment," horizontal picture with woman holding flowers and a bottle of Coke, 1950s, 50" x 29", EX, $350.00 C.

Poster, cardboard, "Home Refreshment on the Way," extremely attractive young woman wearing a wide-brimmed hat and carrying a basket of Coke, 1940s, 24½" x 50", VG, $650.00 B. *Metz Superlatives Auction.*

Poster, cardboard, "Home Refreshment" with a pretty girl sitting talking to a man in military uniform, 1944, EX, $1,300.00 B. *Metz Superlatives Auction.*

Poster, cardboard, "Home Refreshment," young woman in front of an open refrigerator, holding a bottle of Coke, 1950s, 16" x 27", NM, $550.00 B. *Metz Superlatives Auction.*

Poster, cardboard, "It's a Family Affair," family enjoying a Coke, Canadian, 1941, EX, $400.00 B. *Metz Superlatives Auction.*

Poster, cardboard, Kit Carson, promotional item for the TV cowboy, with a six-pack the buyer could get an official kerchief, 1950s, 16" x 24", EX, $225.00 B.

Poster, cardboard, "James Brown," with psychedelic artwork, hard to locate this one, 1960s, 16" x 27", EX, $200.00 B. *Metz Superlatives Auction.*

Poster, cardboard, "Join Me," young lady fencing contestant resting on a store cooler with a cold bottle of Coke, 16" x 27", EX, $775.00 B. *Metz Superlatives Auction.*

Poster, cardboard, "Let's Have a Coke," young lady majorette sitting on top of a store cooler, 16" x 27", EX, $395.00 C.

Poster, cardboard, "Lunch Refreshed," working men and woman taking their lunch break, 1943, EX, $1,000.00 B. *Metz Superlatives Auction.*

Poster, cardboard, "Lunchez rafraichi," vertical, pretty girl with hat and a bottle of Coke, French Canadian, 1948, 16" x 27", EX, $850.00 B. *Metz Superlatives Auction.*

Poster, cardboard, "Me, Too!" young bright eyed boy eager for a bottle of Coke, 62" x 33", G, $525.00 C.

Poster, cardboard, "Mind Reader," pretty girl sunning and being handed a bottle of Coke, 1960s, EX, $650.00 C. *Metz Superlatives Auction.*

Poster, cardboard, "Pause and Refresh" with pretty girl sitting a soda fountain with dispenser, 1948, 41" x 23½", NM, $2,300.00 B. *Metz Superlatives Auction.*

Poster, cardboard, "Pause...Refresh... Drink Coca-Cola," vertical, bottle in festive background, Canadian, framed and under glass, 1949, 16" x 27", EX, $425.00 B. *Metz Superlatives Auction.*

Poster, cardboard, "On the Refreshing Side," couple with bottles of Coke at sporting event, 1941, 30" x 50", VG, $600.00 B. *Metz Superlatives Auction.*

Poster, cardboard, "Pause," with skating scene and clown, still in an original factory frame, 1930s, EX, $850.00 B – 925.00 D. *Metz Superlatives Auction.*

Poster cardboard, "Play
Host to Thirst," vertical,
friends around a large
tub of iced Cokes, 1950s,
16" x 27", EX, $375.00 B.
Metz Superlatives Auction.

Poster, cardboard, "Play Refreshed,"
woman on carousel horse, still in original factory frame, 1940s, EX,
$1,200.00 B. *Metz Superlatives Auction.*

Poster, cardboard, "Refresh" with pretty
majorette about to enjoy a bottle of Coke,
1952, G, $325.00 D.

Poster, cardboard,
"Refresh Yourself" with
horses and riders,
1957, 16" x 27", VG,
$425.00 D.

Poster, cardboard, "Ride Along," Dale Earnhardt and a Coke store advertising, 36" x 46", EX, $35.00 – 55.00 C.

Poster, cardboard, "Round the World 1944," die-cut lady in heavy coat with a glass of Coke, framed, 1944, EX, $325.00 D. *Riverside Antique Mall.*

Poster, cardboard, "Serve Yourself" with glass in hand, 1949, 13" x 11", NM, $170.00 B. *Metz Superlatives Auction.*

Poster, cardboard, "Serves 3 Over Ice – Nice...Drink Coca-Cola...Big 16 oz. Size," horizontal with a lady at kitchen table, 1950s, 27" x 16", EX, $350.00 B. *Metz Superlatives Auction.*

Poster, cardboard, skiers in winter snow scene, "Be Really Refreshed," in metal frame, 1955, 36" x 20", EX, $335.00 C.

Poster, cardboard, "So Delicious," woman in heavy winter coat with hood, 1950s, VG, $475.00 B. *Metz Superlatives Auction.*

Poster, cardboard, "So Easy," hostess preparing for the party by candlelight, 1950s, VG, $495.00 C.

Poster, cardboard, "Start Refreshed," couple at roller skating rink, man in Naval uniform, two bottles of Coke, 1943, 16" x 27", EX, $425.00 C.

Poster, cardboard,
"Take Coke Along,"
young couple pic-
nicking with basket
and cooler of ice-cold
Cokes, 1951,
16" x 27", EX,
$700.00 B. *Metz
Superlatives Auction.*

Poster, cardboard, "Stop...Go
Refreshed," glass of Coke and
1950s-style steering wheel,
1950s, 16" x 27", VG, $295.00 C.

Poster, cardboard, "Talk about Refreshing,"
young ladies on beach with bottles of Coke,
1943, VG, $800.00 B. *Metz
Superlatives Auction.*

Poster, cardboard, "Take
Home a Carton...Easy to
Carry" with woman carrying
a carton of Cokes, 1937,
14" x 32", EX, $1,600.00 B.
Metz Superlatives Auction.

Poster, cardboard, "Talk about
Refreshing," young lady with
umbrella and a bottle of Coke
in front of a store cooler, 1942,
EX, $600.00 C.

Poster, cardboard, "The Best
is Always the Better Buy," girl
carrying a bag of groceries and
a six-pack carton of Coke,
1943, EX, $975.00 B. *Metz
Superlatives Auction.*

Poster, cardboard, "The Pause That Refreshes at Home,"
woman sitting with bottle and six-pack in background, VG,
$675.00 C. *Mitchell Collection.*

Poster, cardboard, "The Pause That Refreshes," three workers around a cooler, vertical version, 1940s, EX, $375.00 D.

Poster, cardboard, "The Pause That Refreshes," young lady tennis player being handed a bottle of Coke, vertical version, 1943, EX, $500.00 B. *Metz Superlatives Auction.*

Poster, cardboard, "The Pause That Refreshes," woman on beach in swimsuit, 1950s, 36" x 20", G, $375.00 C.

Poster, cardboard, "Things Go Better with Coke," couple roller skating, 1960s, EX, $140.00 B. *Metz Superlatives Auction.*

Poster, cardboard, "Things Go Better with Coke," scene of food platter and bottle of Coke, 1960s, F, $145.00 D.

Poster, cardboard, "Thirst Knows No Season" couple building large snowman, 1942, 30" x 50", NM, $775.00 C.

Poster, cardboard, "To Be Refreshed," with woman with a Coke bottle in each hand, EX, $495.00 C.

Poster, cardboard, "Welcome Friend," lettering on background designed to resemble simulated oak, 1957, 14" x 12", EX, $375.00 C. *Mitchell Collection.*

Poster cardboard, "Welcome Home," woman reaching for a couple of bottles of Coke and talking to a man in uniform, 1944, 36" x 20", EX, $450.00 C.

Poster, cardboard, "Welcome Pause," young lady tennis player enjoying a bottle of Coke, 1942, 30" x 50", NM, $795.00 C.

Poster, cardboard, "Wherever You Go," travel
scenes and a cold bottle of Coke, 1950s, EX,
$325.00 C. *Mitchell Collection.*

Poster, cardboard, "Yes," girl on beach being offered a bottle of Coke,
horizontal version, 1946, 56" x 27", EX, $625.00 C. *Mitchell Collection.*

Poster, cardboard, "Yield to the Children," kids in
street crossing, truck size ad, 1960s, 67" x 32",
EX, $115.00 C.

Poster, paper, "Drink...Delicious and Refreshing..." framed, under glass, 1890 – 1900s, VG, $1,500.00 B.

Poster, paper, "Let's Have a Coke," couple in uniform, 1930s, 57" x 20", G, $850.00 B. *Mitchell Collection.*

Poster, paper, Ritz Boy used for the first time, "60,000,000 Drinks a Day," 1920s, F, $735.00 C. *Mitchell Collection.*

Poster, paper, "Pause a Minute...Refresh Yourself" with pretty girl and a bottle, 1927 – 1928, 12" x 20", EX, $1,800.00 B. *Metz Superlatives Auction.*

Poster, paper, "Which." This item has been trimmed; that has eliminated the wording. Pretty girl with a straight-sided bottle in one hand and Goldelle Ginger Ale in the other. If this were in mint condition the value would be doubled, 1905, G, $4,900.00 C.
Mitchell Collection.

Rack mount, cardboard, with diamond cans, 1960s, NM, $85.00 D.

Rack mount, metal, "Things Go Better with Coke...Drink Coca-Cola...Please Place Empties Here," rolled edges for bottle rack, 1960s, 14½" x 5", VG, $135.00 C.

Trolley car, cardboard, "Get It With Your Groceries," scene of a six-pack carton in a woven hand-carried basket, 1930s, 21" x 11", EX, $1,300.00 B. *Metz Superlatives Auction.*

Sidewalk, metal, "Drink Coca-Cola...Ice Cold," fishtail sidewalk sign, 1960s, 22½" x 33", EX, $500.00 C.

Trolley car, cardboard, "Good Company" with a toast being presented with Coke glasses, 1927, 21" x 11", EX, $3,000.00 B. *Metz Superlatives Auction.*

Trolley car, cardboard, "The Drink Everyone Knows" with winged button saying "Pause...Go Refreshed," 1941, 21" x 11", EX, $1,150.00 B. *Metz Superlatives Auction.*

Trolley car, cardboard, "Drink Coca-Cola Delicious and Refreshing," matted, framed and under glass, 1914, 21" x 11", F – EX, $800.00 C – $3,400.00 C. *Mitchell Collection.*

Wall hung, porcelain, "Drug Store...Drink Coca-Cola...Delicious and Refreshing," horizontal and very heavy, 8' x 5', EX, $1,200.00 D.

Window display, cardboard, "Drink Coca-Cola," with endorsements by Jackie Coogan and Wallace Berry with tall Coke bottle in center, 1934, 43" x 32", EX, $7,700.00 B.
Metz Superlatives Auction

Button, metal, "Buvez Coca-Cola," French Canadian, 12" dia., EX, $350.00 B. *Metz Superlatives Auction.*

Button, metal, "Drink Coca-Cola," 1950s, 12" dia., VG, $150.00 B. *Metz Superlatives Auction.*

Button, metal, "Drink Coca-Cola...Sign of Good Taste," two-color lettering, 1953, 24" dia., EX, $475.00 B.

Button, metal, "Drink Coca-Cola," made in and for use in U.S.A., 1957, 16" dia., EX, $475.00 B.

Button, metal, "Drink Coca-Cola" with metal arrow, 1960s, 18" dia., VG, $775.00 C.

Display, celluloid, "Coca-Cola," round disc with bottle, 1950s, 9" dia., EX, $295.00 C.

Display, metal, "Drink Coca-Cola," round iron frame with button on each side in center, 24" dia., VG, $1,100.00 C.

Display, metal, "Please Pay Cashier," built to back light the center disc, 1930s, 12" x 14", EX, $2,600.00 B. *Metz Superlatives Auction.*

Display, metal and plastic, "Drink Coca-Cola...Sign of Good Taste," light-up disc-type sign, 1950s, 16" dia., EX, $495.00 C. *Mitchell Collection.*

Back bar, cardboard, "Drink Coca-Cola," framed, under glass, 1918, 96" long, EX, $4,500.00 B. *Metz Superlatives Auction.*

Back bar, cardboard, Autumn Leaves, five pieces, woman with glass of Coke and colorful fall leaves, 1927, G, $1,000.00 B. *Metz Superlatives Auction.*

Back bar, cardboard, "Know Your State Tree," in original envelope, 1950s, EX,
$750.00 – 850.00 C. *Mitchell Collection.*

Back bar, cardboard, "Drink Coca-Cola," woman with glass of Coke, in original envelope, five pieces, 1937, EX, $4,000.00 B. *Metz Superlatives Auction.*

Back bar, cardboard, "Snowman," Canadian piece featuring a snowman with a fountain attendant's hat, five pieces, 1936, 14', EX, $7,500.00 B. *Metz Superlatives Auction.*

Back bar, cardboard, "Swans," 1930s, EX, $1,500.00 B.
Metz Superlatives Auction.

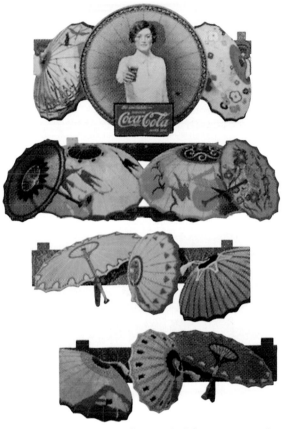

Back bar, cardboard, "Parasols," five pieces with
centerpiece featuring a pretty girl with an extended
glass of Coke, 1927, G, $4,700.00 B. *Metz Superlatives
Auction.*

Back bar, masonite, "Howdy Pardner," three pieces with the message
"Pause...Refresh," EX, $850.00 B. *Metz Superlatives Auction.*

Back bar, plywood and metal, "Weidelich Pharmacies," super item used until the stores closed in the 1960s, 36" x 20" center, 36" x 18" ends, G, $4,000.00 B. *Metz Superlatives Auction.*

Back bar, cardboard, "Orchids," "The Pause That Refreshes," five pieces, 1941, 12' long, EX, $1,300.00 B. *Metz Superlatives Auction.*

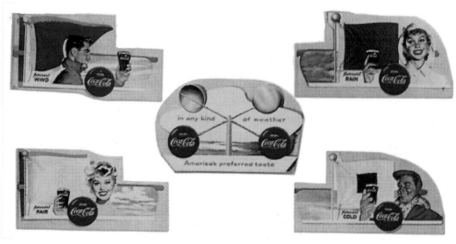

Back bar, cardboard, "Weather," five pieces with different weather scenes, approx. 10' long, EX, $1,200.00 B. *Metz Superlatives Auction.*

Hanging, metal, "Drink Coca-Cola in Bottles" on button on top, 1950s, 8" x 19", EX, $415.00 B. *Metz Superlatives Auction.*

Hanging, paper, "America, Love It or Leave It," advertising from Brownsville, TN, with a display of a drum and fife scene, full monthly pads, 1942, EX, $155.00 C. *Mitchell Collection.*

Hanging, paper, baseball girl with glass, scene of early baseball game in background, matted, framed and under glass, 1922, 12" x 32", NM, $2,200.00 C. *Mitchell Collection.*

Hanging, paper, boy with fishing pole and a couple of bottles of Coke, matted, framed and under glass, 1937, 12" x 24", M, $875.00 C. *Mitchell Collection.*

Hanging, paper, "Coca-Cola," Betty top only, rare version featured with a straight-sided bottle and a straw, 1914, VG, $2,500.00 C.

Hanging, paper, "Coca-Cola," girl with racquet, from Asa Chandler & Co., tear pad at bottom has been moved for better view of calendar, 1891, G, $5,500.00 C.

Hanging, paper, "Coke Has the Taste You Never Get Tired of," pretty girl with a bottle of Coke and a 45rpm record, double-month display, full pad, 1968, M, $90.00 C.
Mitchell Collection.

Hanging, paper, "Coke Refreshes You Best," lady being offered a bottle of Coke, double-month display, full pad, 1961, M, $100.00 C. *Mitchell Collection.*

Hanging, paper, "Drink Coca-Cola...Delicious and Refreshing," original metal strip on top, full monthly pad, 1914, VG, $1,750.00 C.

Hanging, paper, "Drink Coca-Cola Delicious Refreshing," woman drinking from a glass with syrup line, 1913, 13" x 22", VG, $2,700.00 C.

Hanging, paper, "Drink Delicious Coca-Cola," Coca-Cola girl with big-brimmed hat, full monthly sheets, matted, framed and under glass, 1911, 10" x 17", M, $4,900.00 D.

Hanging, paper, Elaine the World War I girl holding a glass, incorrect pad, 1916, 13" x 32", NM, $2,300.00 C.

Hanging, paper, "Drink Coca-Cola" top only, still has the top metal strip, pretty girl with glass in hand and one on the table, lighted building in background from World Exposition, 1909, 11" x 14", EX, $5,500.00 B. *Metz Superlatives Auction.*

Hanging, paper, girl in coat with a bottle of Coke, double-month display, 1948, EX, $450.00 C. *Mitchell Collection.*

Hanging, paper, girl in tennis outfit with bright red scarf, holding a glass of Coke with a bottle on the table, matted, framed and under glass, 1926, 10" x 18", VG, $1,195.00 C. *Mitchell Collection.*

Hanging, paper, girl in sheer dress with a glass of Coke, message panel for Taylor's Billiard Parlor, matted, framed and under glass, 1927, 12" x 24", M, $1,895.00 C. *Mitchell Collection.*

Hanging, paper, girl pouring Coke from bottle to glass, matted, framed and under glass, 1939, 12" x 24", M, $675.00 C. *Mitchell Collection.*

Hanging, paper; girl smiling, in period dress and holding a glass of Coke while a bottle is sitting on the table; matted, framed and under glass, *beware of reproductions,* 1924, 12" x 24", M, $1,495.00 D. *Mitchell Collection.*

Hanging, paper, girl with ice skates and sitting on a log, displays two months at one time, 1941, EX, $450.00 C. *Mitchell Collection.*

Hanging, paper, girl with shawl and with a bottle of Coke and a straw, matted, framed and under glass, 1923, 12" x 24", VG, $1,100.00 C. *Mitchell Collection.*

Hanging, paper, Knitting Girl with bottle of Coke, partial monthly pad, framed and under glass, 1919, 13" x 32", EX, $3,200.00 D. *Mitchell Collection.*

Hanging, paper, pretty blond girl with snow skis, two-month display, 1947, EX, $475.00 C. *Mitchell Collection.*

Hanging, paper, pretty woman with a bottle of Coke, outdoor scene in background, double months shown on each page, 1944, EX, $395.00 C. *Mitchell Collection.*

Hanging, paper, pretty girl in red hat with bottle of Coke, double-month display, 1949, M, $325.00 C. *Mitchell Collection.*

Hanging, paper, "The Pause That Refreshes," woman looking at clothes in a door mirror, double-month display, full pad, 1963, M, $100.00 C. *Mitchell Collection.*

Hanging, paper, "Things Go Better with Coke," couple relaxing by a log cabin, each with a bottle of Coke, double-month display, full pad, 1965, M, $100.00 C. *Mitchell Collection.*

Hanging, paper, "Things Go Better with Coke," young couple at cafe table, double month display, full monthly pads, 1969, M, $85.00 C. *Mitchell Collection.*

Hanging, plastic, "Drink Coca-Cola...Coke Refreshes You Best," fishtail top design, bottom daily tear sheets, all sheets present, 1960s, EX, $475.00 B. *Metz Superlatives Auction.*

Hanging, paper, canoe and a woman in a swimsuit and holding a bottle, matted, framed and under glass, partial pad, 1930, 12" x 24", M, $1,275.00 C. *Mitchell Collection.*

Pocket, paper, "Tastes Like Home," with sailor and all months shown on front, 1943, EX, $75.00 C. *Mitchell Collection.*

Commerative, metal, "Enjoy Coca-Cola...Bottling Company of Cape Cod...Grand Opening June 1984...45th Anniversary...June 1939 – 1984," with the "Four Seasons Girls" on front, deep lip, 1984, 15" x 12¼", EX, $45.00 C. *B. J. Summers.*

Serving, metal, "Coca-Cola," Garden Girl with a flare glass featuring a flare line, 1920, 10½" x 13¼", EX, $975.00 C. *Mitchell Collection*

Serving, metal, "Coca-Cola...Have a Coke," red hair beauty with a yellow scarf and a bottle of Coke. *Caution — these seem to have reproduced by the tons, 1950s,* 10½" x 13¼", EX, $250.00 C. *Mitchell Collection.*

Serving, metal, "Coca-Cola," Smiling Girl holding a glass of Coke, this tray can have either a brown or maroon border, 1924, 10½" x 13¼", EX, $825.00 C. *Mitchell Collection.*

Serving, metal, "Coca-Cola," Summer Girl with flare glass featuring syrup line, mfg. by H.D. Beach Company, Coshocton, Ohio, 1922, 10½" x 13¼", EX, $900.00 C. *Mitchell Collection.*

Serving, metal, "Drink Coca-Cola at Soda Fountains 5¢," Lillian Nordica with a glass of coke on table, 1905, 10½" x 13", EX, $4,500.00 D.

Serving, metal, "Drink Coca-Cola," another American Art Works product with pretty girl in yellow swimsuit and with a bottle of Coke, 1929, 10½" x 13¼", EX, $800.00 C. *Mitchell Collection.*

Serving, metal, "Drink Coca-Cola"
bobbed-hair girl drinking Coke
through a straw from a bottle,
1928, 10½" x 13¼", EX, $825.00 C.
Mitchell Collection.

Serving, metal, "Drink Coca-Cola,"
boy and dog at fishing hole eating
lunch, 1931, 10½" x 13¼", EX,
$1,100.00 D. *Mitchell Collection.*

Serving, metal, "Drink Coca-Cola...Deli-
cious and Refreshing," girl on springboard
with a bottle of Coke, 1939, 10½" x 13¼",
EX, $400.00 C. *Mitchell Collection.*

Serving, metal, "Drink Coca-Cola...Deli-
cious and Refreshing,"
pretty young lady with sailor hat fishing
from a dock and enjoying a bottle of
Coke, 1940, 13¼" x 10½", NM, $625.00 B.
Buffalo Bay Auction Co.

Serving, metal, "Drink Coca-Cola," French, with food and Coke bottles on table, 1957, 13¼" x 10½", EX, $125.00 C. *Mitchell Collection.*

Serving, metal, "Drink Coca-Cola," Garden Girl with flare glass, oval shaped, 1920, 13¼" x 16½", EX, $925.00 C. *Mitchell Collection.*

Serving, metal, "Drink Coca-Cola," girl in swimsuit and red cap with a bottle of Coke, 1930, 10½" x 13¼", EX, $525.00 C. *Mitchell Collection.*

Serving, metal, "Drink Coca-Cola," girl in yellow swimsuit running on beach with bottle of Coke in each hand, 1937, 10½" x 13¼", EX, $425.00 C. *Mitchell Collection.*

Serving, metal, "Drink Coca-Cola...Have a Coke...Thirst Knows No Season," commonly known as the Menu Girl, tray was produced in different languages, 1950 – 1960s, 10½" x 13¼", VG, $95.00 C.
B. J. Summers.

Serving, metal, "Drink Coca-Cola...in Bottles 5¢...at Fountains 5¢," with Juanita drinking Coke from a flare glass, 1906, 10½" x 13¼", EX, $2,800.00 D.

Serving, metal, "Drink Coca-Cola...'Meet Me at the Soda Fountain,'" pretty girl on telephone, 1930, 10½" x 13¼", EX, $600.00 C.
Mitchell Collection.

Serving, metal, "Drink Coca-Cola," pretty girl in swimsuit in chair on beach with a bottle of Coke, 1932, 10½" x 13¼", EX, $725.00 C.
Mitchell Collection.

Serving, metal, "Drink Coca-Cola," two pretty women with Cokes beside a vintage car; due to the demand for metal during WWII, this was the last metal tray produced until the war ended; 1942, 10½" x 13¼", EX, $500.00 C. *Mitchell Collection.*

Serving, metal, "Drink Coca-Cola," with the Afternoon Girl holding a bottle of Coke, manufactured by American Art Works, Inc., Coshoctin, Ohio, 1938, 10½" x 13¼", EX, $425.00 C. *Mitchell Collection.*

Serving, metal, "Drink Delicious Coca-Cola," with a King Coca-Cola girl, first rectangular tray used by Coke by American Art Works, Inc. *Caution — watch for reproductions.* 1909, 10½" x 13¼", EX, $1,300.00 C. *Mitchell Collection.*

Serving, metal, "Here's a Coke for You," there are three different versions of this tray, 1961, 13¼" x 10½", EX, $35.00 D.

Serving-commemorative, metal, "Coca-Cola Bottling Company of the Lehigh Valley," with plant in tray center, 1981, EX, $25.00 C. *Mitchell Collection.*

Serving-commemorative, metal, "Drink Coca-Cola," Alabama/Auburn, 1975, EX, $35.00 C. *Mitchell Collection.*

Tip, metal, "Drink Coca-Cola... Delicious! Refreshing!" Hilda Clark at table with a glass of coke, 1900, 6" dia., EX, $3,750.00. C. *Metz Superlatives Auction.*

Tip, metal, "Coca-Cola" with Hilda Clark holding a glass of Coke in a silver holder, 1903, 6" dia., EX, $2,500.00 D.

Tip, metal, "Drink Coca-Cola...Delicious Refreshing," with Betty in white bonnet, 1914, 4⅛" x 6⅜", EX, $625.00 B.

Tip, metal, "Drink Coca-Cola"; with Elaine, also known as the World War I girl, with a glass of Coke; 1916, 4⅜" x 6⅛", EX, $575.00 C.

Tip, metal, "Drink Delicious Coca-Cola," with the Hamilton King Coke girl in wide brim hat, 1910, 4¼" x 6", EX, $775.00 D.

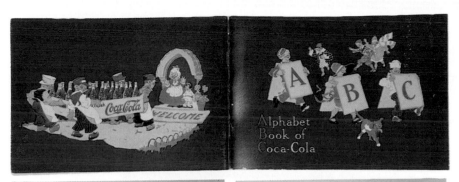

Book, children's, paper, *Alphabet Book of Coca-Cola*, 1928, EX, $120.00 C.
Mitchell Collection.

Book cover, paper, "America is Strong...Because America is Good," U.S. map and Dwight Eisenhower on front, 1950s, EX, $20.00 C. *Mitchell Collection.*

Book cover, paper, "It's the Real Thing" on back, front shows armed forces rank insigias, 1940s, EX, $35.00 C. *Mitchell Collection.*

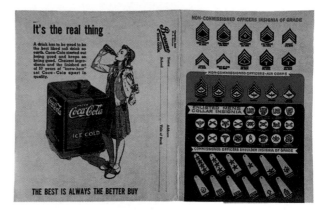

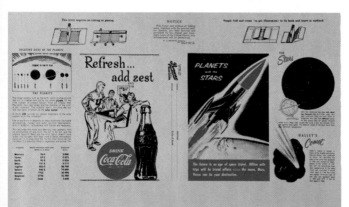

Book cover, paper, "Refresh...Add Zest," front cover has planets and space with rocket blasting off, 1960s, EX, $35.00 C. *Mitchell Collection.*

Border, corrugated paper, "Enjoy Coca-Cola
Classic," 6" tall, EX, $45.00 C.

Border, corrugated paper, "Diet Coke Uncapped," used to
promote the 38th Grammy Awards,
97" x 12", EX, $50.00 C.

Border, corrugated paper, "Enjoy Coca-Cola Classic...Major
League Baseball," EX, $40.00 C.

Border, corrugated paper, "Enjoy Coca-Cola," with advertising
for Super Bowl XXXI, 1991, EX, $40.00 C.

Border, corrugated paper, "Kick Off Your Party with Kraft Foods
and Coca-Cola Products," for Super Bowl XXXV, EX, $45.00 C.

Check, paper, "Coca-Cola Bottling Co.
No. 1" written on the Globe Bank &
Trust Co., Paducah, KY, and signed by
the owner and bottler, Luther Carson,
1908, EX, $110.00 C. *Mitchell Collection.*

Check, paper, "Globe Bank and Trust
Co." This was signed by the Paducah, KY,
bottler, Luther F. Carson; a
signature other than the plant owner
would reduce the value. 1907, EX,
$95.00 C. *Mitchell Collection.*

Coupon, paper, "Pause & Refresh...Drink Coca-Cola in Bottles," good for a 5¢ bottle, VG, $20.00 C.

Coupon, cardboard, "Save This Valuable Coupon," 1940 – 1950s, EX, $8.00 – 10.00 C. *B. J. Summers.*

Coupon, cardboard, "This Ticket is Good for ONE FREE CUP of Coca-Cola," 1940 – 1950s, EX, $8.00 – 10.00 C. *B. J. Summers.*

Coupon, cardboard, "Enjoy These 6 Bottles with Our
Compliments," woman at table with a six-pack carton,
1930 – 1940s, EX, $10.00 – 15.00 C. *B. J. Summers.*

Coupon, cardboard, "You Are Cordially Invited to Accept This Carton
Free When You Buy This One," 1950s, EX, $8.00 – 10.00 C.
B. J. Summers.

Invitation, paper, Paducah, KY,
new bottling plant opening,
1939, EX, $45.00 C.
Mitchell Collection.

Menu sheet, paper, "Things Go Bet-
ter with Coke," plastic holder, 1960s,
EX, $55.00 C.
Mitchell Collection.

Notebook, paper, "Drink Coca-
Cola...Pure as Sunlight," 1930s, VG,
$35.00 C. *Metz Superlatives Auction.*

Placemat, paper, "There's Nothing Like a Coke," football scene in rear, double sided, 1960s, EX, $8.00 – 10.00 C. *B. J. Summers.*

Safety card, paper, "Central States 1996...Safety...Pour It On!!!!" employee item, EX, $5.00 C.

Poster pasted on sheets, paper, "Steel...a Modern Essential," educational items with fantastic colors and material for classroom use, demand seems to be slowly rising on items but is still low in comparison to other Coke advertising, 1940 – 1950s, EX, $50.00 – 75.00 C. *B. J. Summers.*

Bamboo, "Keep Cool, Drink Coca-Cola," with Oriental scene on one side and message on other side, VG, $235.00 C. *Mitchell Collection.*

Solid back, bamboo, church fan donated by the Ruston, LA, Coca-Cola bottler, 1920s, EX, $145.00 C. *Mitchell Collection.*

Solid back, bamboo, "Drink Coca-Cola...Refresh Yourself," Waycross, GA, 1950s, EX, $100.00 C. *Mitchell Collection*

Solid back, cardboard, "Buy by the Carton," from the Memphis, TN, bottler, 1930s, EX, $195.00 C.

Solid back, cardboard, "Drink Coca-Cola," featuring a yellow spotlighted bottle, wooden handle, 1930s, EX, $155.00 C. *Mitchell Collection.*

Solid back, cardboard, "Drink Coca-Cola" on colored background with yellow spotlighted bottle, wooden handle, 1930s, EX, $100.00 C. *Mitchell Collection.*

Solid back, cardboard, "Drink Coca-Cola," with a poem named "Jackie" on the back, 1930s, EX, $225.00 C.

Solid back, cardboard, "Drink Coca-Cola," with dynamic wave logo, wooden handle, from the Coca-Cola Bottling Works of Greenwood, MS, 1960s, EX, $40.00 C.

103

Cardboard, "Be Prepared...Be Refreshed," young Boy Scout at box cooler with a couple of Coke bottles. This blotter crosses collectible lines — Coke, Boy Scouts, and coolers — so it will be sought after by more than just Coke collectors, 1940s, M, $350.00 B.

Cardboard, "Drink Coca-Cola in Bottles... 'Good,' " with Sprite Boy in bottle cap hat, 7¼" x 3½", EX, $35.00 C.

Cardboard, "Drink Coca-Cola...Restores Energy...Strengthens the Nerves," 1926, EX, $145.00 C.

Cardboard, "Friendliest Drink on Earth," bottle in hand in front
of world globe, 1956, 8" x 4", NM, $50.00 D.

Cardboard, "Good with Food...Try It," sandwich plate
and bottles of Coke, 1930s, NM, $75.00 D. *Collectors
Auction Services.*

Cardboard, "The Pause That Refreshes," pretty woman with
Coke bottle seated on ground with blanket, 1934,
EX, $100.00 D.

Paper, "Coca-Cola...Delicious...Refreshing," scene of Piccadilly Circus London, with large Coke advertisement on the side of building, EX, $25.00 C.
Metz Superlatives Auction.

Paper, "Coca-Cola Bottling Co., No. 1," postally used card with vignette of Coke bottling plant. The number *1* on this card refers to the first plant this bottler opened; later he opened and licensed many others. 1920s, EX, $95.00 C.
Mitchell Collection.

Paper, "Coca-Cola," scene of the Coke pavilion at the 1964 World's Fair in New York, 1964, 5½" x 3½", EX, $30.00 C.

Paper, "Drink Delicious Coca-Cola," featuring the Hamilton King Coca-Cola girl, 1910, NM, $775.00 B.
Metz Superlatives Auction.

Magazine, paper, "Drink Coca-Cola...Completely Refreshing" with bathing beauty on towel with a bottle of Coke, 1941, 7" x 10", VG, $5.00 – 15.00 C.

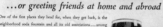

Magazine, paper, "Have a Coca-Cola = Howdy, Neighbor," super WWII *National Geographic* back cover with serviceman in soda fountain relating experiences to a young man with his sister and mother, 1936, 7" x 10", VG, $5.00 – 10.00 C.

Magazine, paper, "Drink Coca-Cola," from back page of *National Geographic*. This is one of the better ads in my opinion; it has a couple projecting the wholesome Coke image, they're in front of a highly sought-after vending machine, the Coke disc (button) is very visible, Sprite Boy is in the image, there is line promoting "Coke Time" with Eddie Fisher on television, and to remind us how good it is, there is the slogan "The Pause That Refreshes...Fifty Million Times a Day." 1955, 7" x 10", VG, $5.00 – 15.00 C.

Magazine, paper, "Drink Coca-Cola...Get the *Feel* of Wholesome Refreshment," bottle in hand and glacier with "wet box" machine, 1936, 7" x 10", VG, $5.00 – 15.00 C.

Magazine, paper, "So Easy to Take Home the Six-bottle Carton" with small girl on grocery counter with a vintage cardboard carrier, small black and white insert showing Mom putting the bottles in the fridge to cool, 1949, 7" x 10", VG, $5.00 – 10.00 C.

Magazine, paper, "Stretch and Refresh...Have a Coca-Cola," scene with stadium vendor at ball game, 1949, 7" x 10", VG, $5.00 – 8.00 C.

Magazine, paper, "Thru 50 years...1886 – 1936...the Pause That Refreshes," ladies in appropriate swimwear for the times and with bottles of Coke, 1936, 7" x 10", VG, $5.00 – 10.00 C.

Magazine, paper, "Thru 50 years — Making a Pause Refreshing...Drink Coca-Cola...Delicious and Refreshing," soda fountain attendants of the time 1886 – 1936, 1936, 7" x 10", VG, $5.00 – 10.00 C.

Magazine, paper, "Coca-Cola 5¢ Everywhere," front and back cover of the *Housekeeper* with front page of pretty woman drinking from a flare glass in a fountain holder, matted, framed and under glass, 1909, VG, $150.00 C.

Magazine, paper, "Even the Bubbles Taste Better," young boy drinking from a hobbleskirt bottle with bubbles floating around him, 1956, VG, $15.00 C.

Magazine, paper "You Taste Its Quality," from *National Geographic,* pretty girl drinking from a hobbleskirt bottle, 1951, F, $12.00 C.

Book, advertising, paper, bottlers'
price guide for advertising items,
1944, EX, $275.00 B.
Metz Superlatives Auction.

Book, advertising, paper, bottlers'
price list with all the advertising
signs and items available to them,
1943, EX, $235.00 B.
Metz Superlatives Auction.

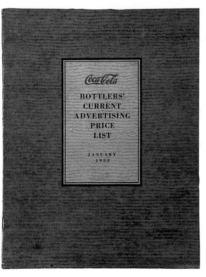

Book, advertisement, paper, bottlers' current prices for advertising
items, 1932, EX, $250.00 C.
Mitchell Collection.

Book, bottler, paper and vinyl, Gold
Service display book for bottler use,
EX, 85.00 C.

Book, history, paper, "Chronological History of the Coca-Cola Company," a very brief history of Coke and its products, VG, $35.00 C.

Book, information kit, paper, heavy stock, spiral-bound refreshment kit for displaying and merchandising effectively, NM, $275.00 C.

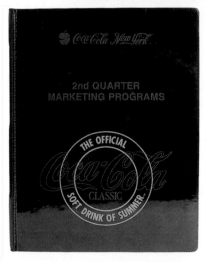

Book, marketing, paper and vinyl, binder with marketing programs for the second quarter, NM, $225.00 C.

Book, merchandising, paper and vinyl, "The Merchandising and Centennial Programs," three-ring binder full of 100th anniversary items for merchandising, 1986, EX, $275.00 C.

Book, material information, paper, heavy stock for five-ring binder with information on the Cooler Radio, 1950s, EX, $80.00 C.
Mitchell Collection.

Book, supplies, paper and vinyl, Paul Flum supply catalog of items needed for advertising, point of purchase to molded fiberglass cooler in shape of older cooler, EX, $75.00 C.

Display, plastic, "Coca-Cola," large hobbleskirt store attention getter, 1953, 20" high, EX, $375.00 B.
Wm. Morford Investment Grade Collectibles.

Hobbleskirt, glass, "100 Years..." commemorative from the Paducah, KY, bottling company, clear, 2003, 8 oz., NM, $5.00 C.
B. J. Summers.

Hobbleskirt, glass, "Coca-Cola 50th Anniversary," gold-dipped limited production bottles on presentation bases, very unusual to find a matched pair, both still have the chain and medallion, plus the wife's bottle has the bracelet, bases are plastic and all four sides are written in gold celebrating with the bottler's name and employee and spouse, finding a matching pair adds to the collector demand and also the value, 1953, 6 oz., EX, $500.00 pair C. *B. J. Summers.*

Hobbleskirt, glass, six in original cardboard carton, with the countdown at one year left until the 1996 Olympics, clear, 1995, EX, $45.00 D. *Pleasant Hill Antique Mall and Tea Room/Bob Johnson.*

Hobbleskirt, glass, tall display model of the Christmas 1923 bottle, in original display box with the original tag around the neck of the bottle with instructions for filling, clear, 1930s, 20" tall, EX, $750.00 B. *Metz Superlatives Auction.*

Hobbleskirt, glass, screw-on top, white lettering in English on one side and foreign on other side, bought by serviceman on overseas duty from a vending machine, Japanese, EX, $20.00 C. *Brian and Christy Kopishke.*

Hobbleskirt miniature, glass, perfume bottle and stopper, *reproductions exist,* clear, 1930s, EX, $85.00 C.

Hobbleskirt commemorative, glass, Super Bowl 2000, in original carton, 2000, 8 oz., NM, $95.00 C.

115

Seltzer, glass, "Coca-Cola Bottling Company...Cairo, Illinois." Another great example of a Cairo bottle, and contrary to most thinking, this one is scarcer than the Ritz Boy Cairo seltzer. Some calcium deposit on inside of bottle that could be cleaned, and a good clean metal top. 1940 – 1950s, EX, $575.00 C. *B. J. Summers.*

Refrigerator, glass, "Compliments Coca-Cola Bottling Co.," water bottle with green glass and advertising on front, EX, $125.00 – 145.00 C. *Mitchell Collection.*

Seltzer, glass, "Property of Cairo, Illinois Coca-Cola Bottling Co.," with Ritz Boy carrying a bottle on a tray, good cap with very little metal distress and a good strong bottle label. This bottler, now out of business, was related to Luther Carson, who founded and operated the Paducah, KY, bottling plant, and the factory (Cairo) obtained its license through the Paducah plant. 1940 – 1950s, EX, $450.00 C. *B. J. Summers.*

Seltzer, glass and metal, "Coca-Cola Bottling Company, Bradford, PA," acid etched, light aqua, EX, $285.00 C.

Seltzer, glass and metal, "Coca-Cola Bottling Works... Clearfield, PA," EX, $165.00 C.

Seltzer, glass and metal, "Northern Coca-Cola Bottling Works, Inc., Messena, N.Y.," EX, $245.00 C.

Straight sided, glass, "Coca-Cola...Bottling Co. No.1...Trade Mark Registered...Paducah, KY," very good slug plate with good embossing, all seams are raised and pronounced, light green, 1903 – 1915, 6.5 oz., EX, $500.00 C.

B. J. Summers.

Straight sided, glass, "Coca-Cola" in script embossed in center with embossed border, aqua, 1910s, 6 oz., VG, $175.00 C.

Straight sided, glass, "Coca-Cola" inside arrow circle, Louisville, KY, light amber, 1910s, 6 oz., EX, $195.00 C.

Straight sided, glass, "Coca-Cola" in script inside of double diamonds, from Toledo, OH, light amber, 1900 – 1910, 6 oz., EX, $195.00 C.

Straight sided, glass, first generation throw-away bottle with embossed diamond, inside is embossed bottle and block "Coke," still full, clear, 1960s, 10 oz., NM, $45.00 C.

Straight sided, glass, "Registered... Coca-Cola...Bottling Co...To Be Returned to Paducah, KY," clear, 1903 – 1915, 6.5 oz., EX, $85.00 C.
B. J. Summers.

Straight sided commemorative, glass, 75th anniversary bottle, with painted facsimile of paper label, clear, 1978, 10 oz., EX, $15.00 – 20.00 C.
B. J. Summers.

Straight sided commemorative, glass, "The Cola Clan...Mid South," made bottle for the third annual Septemberfest in Elizabethtown, KY, clear, 1979, 10 oz., EX, $30.00 C. *B. J. Summers.*

Syrup, glass, "Coca-Cola," with paper label, metal screw-on cap, 1960s, one gal., EX, $12.00 C.
B. J. Summers.

Syrup, glass, "Drink Coca-Cola" inside etched wreath, metal cap, 1910s, EX, $600.00 C.

Dynamic wave, metal, NCAA Final Four commerative 16 oz. can and pin set, 1994, EX, $20.00 B. *Metz Superlatives Auction.*

Straight sided, metal, "Coca-Cola" circle label, syrup can for cruise ship use only, red and white, 1940s, 1 gal., G, $250.00 B. *Metz Superlatives Auction.*

Dynamic wave, waxed paper, "Coca-Cola" on front, prototype that was never put into production, metal top and bottom, 12 oz., EX, $175.00 C.

Dynamic wave, steel, "Coca-Cola Light" pop-top lid, bought from vending machine by U.S. serviceman on overseas duty, never opened, Japanese, 250 ml., EX, $25.00 C. *Brian & Christy Kopischke.*

Straight sided, metal, paper label syrup can, red and white, 1940s, 1 gal., EX, $350.00 D.

Bell, pewter, "Coca-Cola," scarce, 1930s, EX, $375.00 B. *Metz Superlatives Auction.*

Bell, glass, "Drink Coca-Cola 5¢," acid-etched arrow and syrup line, 1912 – 1913, EX, $875.00 B. *Metz Superlatives Auction.*

Flare, glass, "Drink Coca-Cola," etched syrup line, clear, 1910s, EX, $500.00 C. *Mitchell Collection.*

Modified flare, glass, "Coca-Cola," clear, 1926, EX, $250.00 C. *Mitchell Collection.*

Glass holder, "Coca-Cola," silver, 1900, VG, $2,400.00 B. *Metz Superlatives Auction.*

Nut dish, "Coca-Cola," different world scenes, 1960s, 11½" x 11½", EX, $145.00 C.

Sandwich plate, "Drink Coca-Cola...Good with Food," scalloped edge, Wellsville China Co., white, 1940 – 1950s, 7½" dia., VG, $750.00 B. *Metz Superlatives Auction.*

Sandwich plate, "Drink Coca-Cola...Refresh Yourself," bottle and glass in center, 1930s, 8¼" dia., NM, $1,200.00 B. *Metz Superlatives Auction.*

Sandwich plate, "Drink Coca-Cola...Refresh Yourself," bottle and glass in center, Knowles China Co., 1931, 8¼" dia., NM, $775.00 B. *Metz Superlatives Auction.*

Metal, Western Coca-Cola Bottling Co., dark haired lady with a very low drape pose, 1908 – 1912, 9⅞" dia., 16" sq. in frame, EX, $450.00 C.

Metal, Western Coca-Cola Bottling Co., dark-haired lady with red cap, 1908 – 1912, 9⅞" dia., 16" sq. in frame, EX, $475.00 C.

Metal, Western Coca-Cola Bottling Co., pretty brunette with a red scarf in her hair and holding a pink rose, 1908 – 1912, 9⅞" dia., 16" sq. in frame, EX, $500.00 C.

Metal, Western Coca-Cola Bottling Co., dark-haired beauty with very revealing pose for the times, 1908 – 1912, 9⅞" dia., 16" sq. in frame, EX, $450.00 C.

Metal, Western Coca-Cola Bottling
Co., risqué drape pose of a pretty
red-headed woman, 1908 – 1912,
9⅞" dia., 16" sq. in frame, EX,
$500.00 C.

Metal,
Western
Coca-Cola
Bottling Co., with
long-haired beauty in a
drape with her head turned. These were
produced in a shadow box–type frame; however, few of the frames seem to exist today.
1908 – 1912, 9⅞" dia., EX, $495.00 D.

Metal,
Western
Coca-Cola Bottling Co., young auburn-
haired beauty with red adornment in
her hair, 1908 – 1912, 9⅞" dia., 16" sq.
in frame, EX, $450.00 C.

Metal, Western Coca-Cola Bottling
Co., topless long-haired beauty, this is
the one everyone is after, a very popular plate, double the value shown if
the original shadow box is still with
the plate, 1908 – 1912, 9⅛" dia., 16"
sq. in frame, EX, $1,200.00 C.

Pocket, celluloid, "Drink Coca-Cola," featuring Elaine with a straight sided paper label bottle in her hand, 1916, 1¾" x 2¾", G, $225.00 B. *Metz Superlatives Auction.*

Pocket, celluloid, "Wherever You Go You Will Find Coca-Cola at All Fountains 5¢," round, 1900s, G, $950.00 C. *Mitchell Collection.*

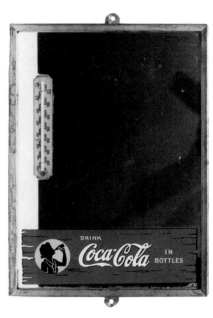

Wall, glass and metal, "Drink Coca-Cola in Bottles," with silhouette girl at bottom and thermometer on left side, 1939, 10" x 14¼", VG, $850.00 B. *Metz Superlatives Auction.*

Wall, glass and wood, "Drink Coca-Cola in Bottles...Coca-Cola Bottling Co. ...Madisonville, KY," arched top, 1920 – 1930s, 8" x 17½", G, $600.00 C. *Mitchell Collection.*

124

Metal, "Drink Coca-Cola," die-cut double-bottle gold version, 1942, 7" x 16", EX, $525.00 C. *Mitchell Collection.*

Wall, cardboard, "Drink Coca-Cola," retailers' reference for regulator settings according to air temperature, 1960s, VG, $75.00 C. *Mitchell Collection.*

Wall, Masonite, "Drink Coca-Cola...Thirst Knows No Season," bottle with tilted scale, 1940s, 6¾" x 17", EX, $500.00 C. *Mitchell Collection.*

Wall, metal, "Drink Coca-cola Delicious and Refreshing" with silhouette girl at bottom of scale, 1930s, 6½" x 16", EX, $500.00 C. *Mitchell Collection.*

Wall, metal, Coca-Cola bottle in oval background, 1938, 6¾" x 16", EX, $350.00 C. *Mitchell Collection.*

Wall, metal, "Drink Coca-Cola...Be Really Refreshed," round dial with fishtail logo in center, 1959, 12" dia., NM, $600.00 B. *Metz Superlatives Auction.*

Wall, metal, "Drink Coca-Cola...Sign of Good Taste...Refresh Yourself," because of the design this is known as the cigar thermometer, 1950s, 8" x 29", EX, $450.00 C.

Wall, metal and glass, "Drink Coca-Cola in Bottles," round dial type reading, 1950s, 12" dia., EX, $250.00 B. *Metz Superlatives Auction.*

Wall, metal and glass, "Drink Coca-Cola...Sign of Good Taste," a round Robertson scale, white on red, 1950s, 12" dia., EX, $150.00 C. *Mitchell Collection.*

Wall, metal and plastic, "Drink Coca-Cola," Pam dial-type scale with red center and green outside ring, 1950s, 12" dia., EX, $475.00 B. *Metz Superlatives Auction.*

Wall, metal and plastic, "Things Go Better with Coke," round Pam with dial type scale reading, 1950s, 12" dia., NM, $250.00 B. *Metz Superlatives Auction.*

Wall, wooden, "Drink Coca-Cola in Bottles...," vertical scale, from V. O. Colson Co., Paris, IL, 1910s, VG, $725.00 C. *Mitchell Collection.*

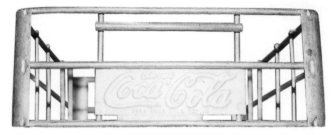

Case, aluminum, "Drink Coca-Cola" on ends, 1940s, 24 bottle, EX, $55.00 C.

Case, 24-bottle, wood, "Refresh Yourself...Drink Coca-Cola in Bottles," very early case with dovetailed joints, 1920s, EX, $295.00 C.

Display rack, metal and wire, "Drink Coca-Cola" disc with three tiers for cartons, unusual and difficult to find, 1940s, F, $290.00 B. *Metz Superlatives Auction.*

Display rack, metal and wire, "Drink Coca-Cola...Take Enough Home," fold-out wire body for store use with metal courtesy panel at top, EX, $175.00 C. *Patrick's Collectibles.*

Display rack, metal and wire, "Take Some Coca-Cola Home Today," wire body with top courtesy panel and metal wheels on bottom, EX, $295.00 C.

Display rack, metal, "Place Empties Here...Thank You," three-case store rack for placement beside a vending machine, G, $425.00 C.

Display rack, metal, "Things Go Better with Coke," miniature sales-man' sample with cases of miniature bottles, 1960s, NM, $2,200.00 B.
Metz Superlatives Auction.

Six-pack, cardboard, "6 for 25¢," 1939, EX, $95.00 C.
Mitchell Collection.

Six-pack, cardboard, "Drink Coca-Cola," straight-sided box with wire handles, 1956, EX, $140.00 C. *Mitchell Collection.*

Six-pack, cardboard, "Season's Greetings...Drink Coca-Cola," with Christmas motif, 1930 – 1940s, VG, $75.00 C. *Mitchell Collection.*

Six-pack, wood, "Pause...Go Refreshed," wire handle with wood grip and wood bottle compartments, wings under message on carton end, 1930s, EX, $450.00 B. *Metz Superlatives Auction.*

Six-pack, wooden, "Drink Coca-Cola in Bottles," wooden cut-out handle, 1940s, EX, $175.00 C. *Mitchell Collection.*

Stadium vendor, metal, "Drink Coca-Cola," metal holder with curved side toward vendors body, insulate, with canvas carrying strap, original opener on end, 1940 – 1950s, VG, $350.00 C. *Mitchell Collection.*

Stadium vendor, metal, "Drink Coca-Cola," backpack with premix device and cup holder, white on red, 1950 – 1960s, G, $525.00 B. *Metz Superlatives Auction.*

Chest, wood and zinc, "Help Yourself...Drink Coca-Cola...Deposit in Box 5¢," very early lined box with side handles and hinged top, red on yellow, 1920s, VG, $325.00 B. *Metz Superlatives Auction.*

Chest, cardboard, "Drink Coca-Cola," Westinghouse WE-6 salesman's sample, 1940 – 1950s, 4⅜" x 4" x 3", G, $475.00 C. *Mitchell Collection.*

Picnic, metal, "Drink Coca-Cola," Acton-produced unit still with original box, metal swing handle, tray is still inside, 1950 – 1960s, 17" x 12" x 19", EX, $395.00 C.

Picnic, metal, "Drink Coca-Cola in Bottles," with swing-type handle and lock, removable top, white on red, 1950s, VG, $145.00 C. *Mitchell Collection.*

Picnic, metal, "Drink Coca-
Cola," airline with round
metal handle on top, 1950s, G,
$325.00 B. *Metz Superlatives
Auction.*

Picnic, metal, "Drink Coca-
Cola," junior stainless steel
with removeable lid and
swing handle lock, 1950s,
12" x 9" x 14", EX, $650.00 B.
Metz Superlatives Auction.

Picnic, metal, "Drink Coca-Cola in Bottles,"
large with message on front, wire handles on
each side, opener on one side at handle,
hinged lift top, G, $135.00 C.

Picnic, metal, "Drink Coca-Cola,"
unusual round design with decal
on outside and zinc liner inside,
white on red, 1940s, 8" x 9", VG,
$250.00 B. *Metz Superlatives Auction.*

Picnic, stainless steel, "Drink Coca-Cola," airline cooler with top embossed "Northwest Airlines," unusual in the short body height, good top handle with snap-down locks, stainless steel, 1940 – 1950s, 9½" tall, EX, $750.00 B. *Metz Superlatives Auction.*

Picnic, metal, "It's the Real Thing...Drink Coca-Cola," dynamic wave logo, wire handles on side with opening top, white on red, 1960s, 18" x 13" x 16½", G, $185.00 D. *Patrick's Collectibles.*

Store, metal and wood, "Serve Yourself...Drink Coca-Cola...Please Pay the Clerk," with original Starr opener and good zinc lining, 32" x 29" x 2¼", F, $1,700.00 B. *Metz Superlatives Auction.*

Store, metal, "Buvez Coca-Cola," foreign with fishtail design logo and two center-hinge top-opening lids that expose the Cokes in one large compartment, 42" x 35" x 27", G, $275.00 B – 350.00 C.

Store, metal, "Drink Coca-Cola," Glascock junior complete with cap catcher, which is a hard-to-locate item, 1929, EX, $2,200.00 C. *Mitchell Collection.*

Store, metal, "Drink Coca-Cola." Two-piece unit — top is picnic cooler and bottom is designed to sit on the floor and accept the top. 1950s, 17" x 12" x 39", EX, $3,100.00 B. *Metz Superlatives Auction.*

Store, metal, salesman's sample of Glascock junior, with the original carrying case, all four side panels with the "Drink Coca-Cola" logo, next to impossible to find in this shape with the original case, 1929, EX, $28,000.00 B. *Metz Superlatives Auction.*

Store, metal, "Serve Yourself...Drink Coca-Cola...Please Pay Cashier," salesman's sample Glascock, complete with miniature cases of bottles on storage rack beneath wet box, NM, $2,300.00 C. *Mitchell Collection.*

Dispenser, metal, with two original sleeves and original box
with mounting instructions, not marked,
6½" x 5", EX, $170.00 B. *Autopia Advertising Auctions.*

Paper, "Drink Coca-Cola...Delicious and Refreshing...a Great Drink...with Good Things to Eat," couple cooking outside and enjoying a bottle of Coke, 1930 – 1940s, 3¾" x 6½", EX, $10.00 – 14.00 C. *B. J. Summers.*

Paper, "Drink Coca-Cola Delicious and Refreshing...Makes a Light Lunch Refreshing," man and woman at lunch counter, 1940s, EX, $15.00 – 20.00 C.

Paper, "Drink Coca-Cola...So Refreshing with Food," woman with cafeteria tray and a bottle of Coke, 1932, VG, $15.00 – 25.00 C. *Mitchell Collection.*

Paper, "Drink Coca-Cola...Delicious and Refreshing...the Drink Everybody Knows," with different version of the bottle in hand, 1930 – 1940s, 3¾" x 6½", EX, $10.00 – 14.00 C.
B. J. Summers.

Paper, "Every Bottle Refreshes...Drink Coca-Cola," 1930 – 1940s, 3¾" x 6½", EX, $6.00 – 8.00 C.
B. J. Summers.

Paper, "It's the Real Thing" pretty lady with bottle of Coke, 1920 – 1930s, 3¾" x 6½", EX, $8.00 – 12.00 C.
B. J. Summers.

Paper, "Now...You Can Buy a Guaranteed Glass — the Distinctive Coca-Cola Glass," hand holding a full Coke glass, EX, $15.00 – 20.00 C.
Metz Superlatives Auction.

Paper, "Quality Carries on...Drink Coca-Cola," bottle in hand, 1930 – 1940s, 3¾" x 6½", EX, $8.00 – 12.00 C.
B. J. Summers.

Paper, "Take Home a Carton...So Easy to Serve at Home," cardboard six-pack, six for 25¢, 1930 – 1940s, 3¾" x 6½", EX, $10.00 – 15.00 C.
B. J. Summers.

Changer, metal, "Drink Coca-Cola...Serve Yourself," made by Vendo Co., with 1938 and 1940 dates, 1940s, 8" x 8½" x 4½", VG, $125.00 – 150.00 C.

Chest, "Drink Coca-Cola," in fishtail logo, Glasco Bottle Vendor dry box, front opener and cap catcher, slider top, Muncie, IN, 1960s, 35½" x 20" x 40", EX, $950.00 – 1,250.00 D.

Chest, metal, "Coca-Cola," decal lettering, lift-top lid, bottle opener and cap catcher, 32" x 18" x 41", F, $700.00 D.

Chest, metal, "Drink Coca-Cola...Ice Cold," Westinghouse ten-case master, top lid hinges in the middle and lifts from both ends, 1950s, 30½" x 36" x 45", NM, $1,850.00 D. *Patrick's Collectibles.*

Chest, metal, "Drink Coca-Cola in Bottles...Ice Cold," Vendo #23, also known as the spin top, found in standard and deluxe models (depends on top and other colors), 1950s, 24" x 36" x 21", EX, $1,395.00 D – 1,695.00 D.

Upright, metal, "Drink Coca-Cola in Bottles," Vendo V-39, very desirable machine due to its small size, also fairly common and easy to find, 1940 – 1950s, 27" x 58" x 16", NM, $2,995.00 D. *Patrick's Collectibles.*

Upright, metal, "Drink Coca-Cola in Bottles," Vendo V-81, a much sought-after machine for home use mostly due to its size and eye appeal, 1950s, 27" x 58" x 16", VG, $1,500.00 C. *Mike and Debbie Summers.*

Upright, metal, "Drink Coca-Cola," Vendolator Dual 27, dispenses 27 bottles, successor to the tabletop machine, 1950s, 25½" x 52" x 17½", NM, $2,295.00 D. *Patrick's Collectibles.*

Upright, metal, Vendo #44, "Drink Coca-Cola," two tone with white top and red bottom, 1950s, 16" x 57½" x 15½", NM, $2,400.00 B – 2,750.00 C. *Metz Superlatives Auction.*

Can, plastic, "Enjoy Coca-Cola" and dynamic wave, 1970s, EX, $50.00 C. *Mitchell Collection.*

Bottle, plastic, "Enjoy Coca-Cola," AM-FM in shape of hobbleskirt bottle, 1970s, EX, $45.00 C. *Mitchell Collection.*

Cooler, plastic and metal, "Coca-Cola Refreshes You Best," an extremely hard-to-locate item, designed to resemble an airline cooler, top lifts to reveal controls, 1950s, G, $3,800.00 B. *Metz Superlatives Auction.*

Vending machine, plastic, "Coke," upright machine, 1980s, EX, $95.00 C. *Mitchell Collection.*

Vending machine, plastic, "Drink Coca-Cola," upright design with left-hand see-through door, 1960s, G, $165.00 C. *Mitchell Collection.*

Radio, vending machine, plastic, "Drink Coca-Cola," upright machine with double drop chute, F, $200.00 C. *Mitchell Collection.*

Vending machine, plastic, "Enjoy Coca-Cola," upright design with dynamic wave panel at top, 1970s, EX, $135.00 C. *Mitchell Collection.*

Counter, metal and glass, "Drink Coca-Cola...Lunch with Us," square clock face at left of message panel, 1940 – 1950s, 19½" x 5" x 9", EX, $950.00 D.

Anniversary, glass and metal, "Drink Coca-Cola" in center of clock face, small miniature bottles on bottom movements, covered by clear glass dome, 1950s, 3" x 5", EX, $975.00 C.
Mitchell Collection.

Desk, china, "Coca-Cola" in red on face, rare and scarce, given to some of the better soda fountains, G, $3,500.00 C.
Mitchell Collection.

Desk, leather, "Drink Coca-Cola in Bottles" with gold lettering and gold hobbleskirt bottle at lower left and right, rare item, 1910, 4⅓" x 6", EX, $1,400.00 C.

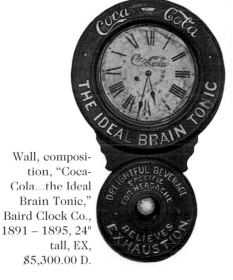

Outside mount, metal, glass and neon, "Drink Coca-Cola...Sign of Good Taste," arched banner from nine to three, 1950s, 36" dia., NM, $1,550.00 B. *Metz Superlatives Auction.*

Wall, composition, "Coca-Cola...the Ideal Brain Tonic," Baird Clock Co., 1891 – 1895, 24" tall, EX, $5,300.00 D.

Wall, metal and wood, "Drink Coca-Cola in Bottles," with extended wings sporting the Sprite Boy decal, 1951, EX, $1,200.00 C.

Wall, metal and glass, "Drink Coca-Cola," in center red dot, 14½" dia., EX, $575.00 C.

143

Wall, metal and glass, "Drink Coca-Cola" with center fishtail logo, green background, NOS, 1960s, EX, $325.00 C.

Wall, metal and glass, neon, "Ice Cold Coca-Cola" with spotlight silhouette girl at bottom of circle, 1940s, 18" x 18", VG, $1,600.00 B. *Metz Superlatives Auction.*

Wall, metal and glass, neon, "Drink Coca-Cola," in center with spotlight bottle at bottom, green wrinkle paint on outside, 1930s, 16" x 16", EX, $825.00 B. *Metz Superlatives Auction.*

Wall, wood and glass, "In Bottles," Gilbert regulator that hung in many bottlers' offices. This one hung in the old location of the Paducah Coca-Cola Bottling Co. office on Jackson St. This clock has only had three owners since the early removal from the Coke office. 1920 – 1930s, EX, $2,100.00 C. *Mitchell Collection.*

Wall, metal and plastic, "Drink Coca-Cola," red and white face, EX, $495.00 C. *Mitchell Collection.*

Handheld, metal,
"Coca-Cola Bottles,"
key style with
Prest-o-lite square
hold in end, EX,
$55.00 D.

Handheld, metal,
"Drink Coca-Cola in
Bottles," brass, key
design with the Prest-
o-lite valve hole,
1910s, EX, $125.00 D.
Mitchell Collection.

Handheld, metal,
"50th Anniversary,"
bottle shaped with
opener on bottom of
bottle, Nashville, TN,
1952, EX, $105.00 C.
Mitchell Collection.

Handheld, metal, "Drink Coca-Cola," nail puller from the
Piqua Coca-Cola Bottling Co., 1960s, EX, $100.00 C.
Mitchell Collection.

Handheld, metal,
"Drink Coca-Cola,"
straight, 1910 – 1950s,
EX, $35.00 – 40.00 C.
Mitchell Collection.

Handheld, metal and plastic, "50th Anniversary Coca-Cola in Bottles," EX, $60.00 C. *Mitchell Collection.*

Handheld, metal and plastic, "75th Anniversary ...Coca-Cola...Coca-Cola Bottling Co., Columbus, Ohio," 1970s, EX, $20.00 C. *Mitchell Collection.*

Handheld, metal and plastic, "Buvez Coca-Cola," red on plastic handle, foreign, EX, $5.00 – 10.00 D. *Collectors Auction Services.*

Wall mounted, metal, corkscrew, 1950s, EX, $45.00 C. *Mitchell Collection.*

Wall mounted, metal, corkscrew, 1920s, EX, $85.00 C. *Mitchell Collection.*

Bulb handle, wood and metal, "Coca-Cola" painted in black on handle, 1920s, VG, $65.00 C. *Mitchell Collection.*

Round handle, wood and metal, bottle opener in handle end, "Coca-Cola in bottles" in red painted lettering on handle, 1930 – 1940s, EX, $40.00 – 45.00 C. *Mitchell Collection.*

Round handle, wood and metal, bottle opener on end of handle, "Drink Coca-Cola in Bottles" in black on handle, 1920 – 1930s, EX, $50.00 C. *Mitchell Collection.*

Square handle, wood and metal, "Coca-Cola in Bottles...Ice-Coal...Phone 87," in painted black lettering on handle, 1930 – 1940s, EX, $35.00 C. *Mitchell Collection.*

Desk, ceramic, "Part-ners...Coca-Cola" with facsmile of baseball in circle, 1950s, 7¼" sq., EX, $85.00 B. *Metz Superlatives Auction.*

Tabletop, ceramic and plastic, "Drink Coca-Cola" logo in bowl, miniature bottle on edge, from Canadian bottler, 1950s, EX, $250.00 B. *Metz Superlatives Auction.*

Tabletop, glass, "Disfrute Coca-Cola" with dynamic wave logo, 1970s, EX, $5.00 – 8.00 D.

Tabletop, metal, "50th Anniversary" embossed with bottle and lettering, Bronze, 1950s, EX, $75.00 – 85.00 C. *Mitchell Collection.*

Ashtray, china, by the Hall China Co. This is a very rare piece. Both sides are pictured to help show both the match holder and the bottle and glass with the message "Refresh Yourself, Drink Coca-Cola," 1930, NM, $5,000.00 C. *Courtesy of Charles Fletcher.*

Tabletop, metal, "Enjoy Coca-Cola" molded cigarette holders and lettering with dynamic wave logo, EX, $35.00 – 40.00 C. *Mitchell Collection.*

Tabletop, metal, "Drink Coca-Cola...High in Quick Energy...Low in Calories," scenes of sports in bowl, 1950s, EX, $30.00 – 35.00 C. *Mitchell Collection.*

Tabletop, glass, set of four different shapes, ruby red glass, price is highest if box is still with set, 1950s, EX, $450.00 – 700.00 C. *Mitchell Collection.*

Pocket, metal, "Drink
Coca-Cola," musical
when lit, 1970s, EX,
$225.00 – 250.00 C.
Mitchell Collection.

Tabletop, metal, "Coke," can
shaped with dynamic wave
contour, 1960 – 1970s, M,
$45.00 – 55.00 C. *Mitchell Col-
lection.*

Pocket, metal and
plastic, in shape of
bottle, fairly common,
1950s, M, $45.00 C.
Mitchell Collection.

Tabletop, metal, "Enjoy
Coca-Cola," in shape of
Coke can with diamond
on front, 1960s, EX,
$45.00 – 65.00 C. *Mitchell
Collection.*

Holder, tabletop, metal, "Drink Coca-Cola...Be *Really* Refreshed!" holder for match books. Books could be pulled out from the bottom and refilled from the top. 1959, EX, $195.00 – 245.00 C. *Mitchell Collection.*

Matchbook, "Coolers for Bottlers of Coca-Cola," G, $8.00 – 10.00 C. *Mitchell Collection.*

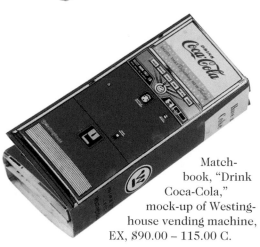

Matchbook, "Drink Coca-Cola," mock-up of Westinghouse vending machine, EX, $90.00 – 115.00 C.

Matchbook, "Have a Coke," 1950s, VG, $5.00 – 10.00 C. *Mitchell Collection.*

Matchbook, "King Size Coke," 1959, VG, $10.00 – 15.00 C. *Mitchell Collection.*

Match safe, pocket, porcelain, "Compliments of Coca-Cola Bottling Co....Union City, Tenn," combination safe and striker, 1930s, EX, $300.00 – 400.00 C. *Mitchell Collection.*

Wall hung, metal, "Drink Coca-Cola in Bottles...Coca-Cola Bottling Co.," 1940s, F, $375.00 – 435.00 C. *Mitchell Collection.*

Wall hung, porcelain, "Drink Coca-Cola Strike Matches Here," 1939, NM, $400.00 B. *Metz Superlatives Auction.*

Wall hung, cardboard, "Drink Coca-Cola...Sign of Good Taste," bottle on each side of message panel, 1959, 19" x 28", NM, $250.00 B. *Metz Superlatives Auction.*

Wall hung, metal, "Drink Coca-Cola," bottle with tag-type panel at top of message area, chalkboard design, EX, $200.00 – 275.00 D. *Riverside Antique Mall.*

Wall hung, metal, "Drink Coca-Cola Delicious and Refreshing," with silhouette girl in lower right corner, American Art Works, Inc., Coshocton, Ohio, 1940s, 19¼" x 27", EX, $275.00 – 400.00 D. *Riverside Antique Mall.*

Wall hung, metal, "Drink Coca-Cola in Bottles" button in center, 1950s, 60" x 14", NM, $2,300.00 B. *Metz Superlatives Auction.*

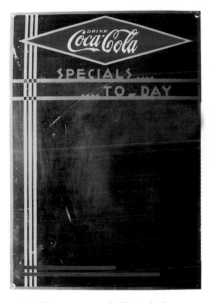

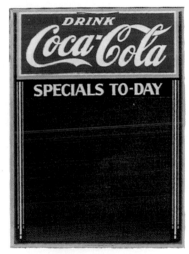

Wall hung, metal, "Drink Coca-Cola...Specials To-day," diamond logo at top, chalk board design, 1931, EX, $300.00 – 450.00 D. *Riverside Antique Mall.*

Wall hung, metal, "Drink Coca-Cola...Specials To-day," product panel at top, chalkboard design, Canadian, difficult to locate, 1938, 17" x 24", NM, $650.00 B. *Metz Superlatives Auction.*

Wall hung, metal, "Specials to-day...Drink Coca-Cola...Refresh Yourself" with bottle and straw in lower right hand corner, 1930s, VG, $325.00 B. *Metz Superlatives Auction.*

Wall hung, plywood, "Drink Coca-Cola...Menu," double rack of menu strips with bottle in center, Kay Displays, 1930s, 36" x 26", G, $375.00 B. *Metz Superlatives Auction.*

Wall hung, wood and metal, "Coca-Cola," Kay Displays, 1940s, F, $550.00 B. *Metz Superlatives Auction.*

Wall hung, wood and metal, "Drink Coca-Cola in Bottles," slide-type menu slots with 16" dia. button at top, Kay Displays, 17" x 29", EX, $525.00 B. *Metz Superlatives Auction.*

Bar, metal, "Coke Adds Life..." unusual black background color,
1970 – 1980s, NM, $75.00 B. *Metz Superlatives Auction.*

Bar, metal, "Drink Coca-Cola delicious refreshing," silhouette girl in yellow spotlight on left side of bar, 1939, 28" x 3½", NM, $500.00 B. *Metz Superlatives Auction.*

Bar, porcelain, "Ice Cold Coca-Cola in Bottles," reverse side has "Thank You, Call Again," 1930s, 25" x 3¼" NM, $475.00 B. *Metz Superlatives Auction.*

Bar, porcelain, "Refreshing Coca-Cola New Feeling," 1950 – 1960s, EX,
$195.00 – 235.00 C. *Mitchell Collection.*

Bar, porcelain, "Take Some Coca-Cola Home Today," 1950s, 34" long, NM,
$525.00 B. *Metz Superlatives Auction.*

Flat plate, porcelain, "Prenez un Coca-Cola," unusual foreign design in horizontal version, 6½" x 3¼", NM, $120.00 B. *Metz Superlatives Auction.*

Flat plate, porcelain, "Come in! Have a Coca-Cola," Canadian, 4" x 11½", NM, $320.00 B. *Metz Superlatives Auction.*

Handle, aluminum, "Drink Coca-Cola," in shape of bottle, 1930s, NM, $275.00 – 300.00 D. *Charlie's Antique Mall.*

Big wheel, metal, "Drink Coca-Cola," delivery vehicle, 1970s, EX, $75.00 – 85.00 C.

Buddy L, metal, "Drink Coca-Coca the Pause That Refreshes!" with original miniature cases and bottles, 1960s, EX, $325.00 – 450.00 C.

Marx, metal, "Drink Coca-Cola Delicious Refreshing," snub-nose cab with full load of cases and bottles, 1950s, VG, $450.00 – 500.00 C.

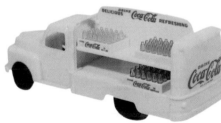

Marx, plastic, "Drink Coca-Cola Delicious Refreshing," Ford style with side load full of cases and bottles, 1950s, EX, $375.00 B. *Metz Superlatives Auction.*

Marx #991, metal, "Coca-Cola...Take Some Home Today" with Sprite Boy in advertising on side panel, gray cab and body with yellow bed, in original box, 1953, NM, $900.00 B. *Metz Superlatives Auction.*

Maxitoys, metal, "Coca-Cola 5¢ at soda fountains," vintage delivery truck made in Holland, only 500 produced, difficult to locate, 1980s, 11" long, NM, $300.00 C.

Metalcraft, metal, "Coca-Cola...Every Bottle Sterlized," rubber tires, with glass bottles on loading bed, 1930s, G, $775.00 C. *Mitchell Collection.*

Model, plastic, "Vending Machine," ½₅ scale, still in plastic sealed box, 1970s, NM, $75.00 – 115.00 C.

Taiyo, metal, "Coca-Cola," metal wind-up, friction motor, in original box, red and white, 1950 – 1960s, 8¾" x 3" x 2", NM, $525.00 B. *Wm. Morford Investment Grade Collectibles.*

Tractor trailer, metal, "Drink Coca-Cola...," red with spotlight carton on trailer, still in box, but the box is less than EX, $225.00 – 245.00 C.

Baseball hall of fame information, cardboard, Coca-Cola premiun, baseball-shaped source of information about the Hall of Fame for both the National and American Leagues, 1901 – 1960, EX, $95.00 B – 150.00 D. *Metz Superlatives Auction.*

Buddy Lee, composition. Doll is in homemade uniform made from an original Coke uniform and patches, all worn by Earlene Mitchell's father when he worked for Coke in Paducah, KY. 1950s, 12" tall, EX, $650.00 C. *Mitchell Collection.*

Puzzle, cardboard, "Coke Adds Life to Everything Nice," potpourri puzzle with over 2,000 pieces in original unopened box, EX, $55.00 – 65.00 C. *Mitchell Collection.*

Roller skates, metal and leather, "Drink Coca-Cola in Bottles...Pat. Aug 16, 1914," thought to be from the St. Louis Bottling Company, 1914, VG, $900.00 B. *Metz Superlatives Auction.*

Shopping basket, metal and cardboard, child's size with products printed on sides, a six-pack of Coca-Cola in plain view and small boxes of products inside basket, 1950s, EX, $450.00 C – 600.00 D. *Mitchell Collection.*

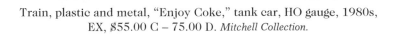

Train, plastic and metal, "Enjoy Coke," tank car, HO gauge, 1980s, EX, $55.00 C – 75.00 D. *Mitchell Collection.*

Can, metal, "Bevete Coca-Cola," dynamic wave logo for the foreign market, top money drop, EX, $95.00 – 115.00 C.

Can, metal, "Coca-Cola" diamond can with top money drop, NM, $85.00 – 95.00 C.

Building, plastic, "You'll Feel Right at Home Drinking Coca-Cola," EX, $135.00 – 165.00 C.

Truck, metal, "Coca-Cola...Advertising Dept." in original box with top coin drop on bed of truck, NM, $35.00 – 65.00 C. *Metz Superlatives Auction.*

Truck, metal, "Drink Coca-Cola...Coca-Cola Bottling Co.," panel design with money drop on top, in original box, NM, $45.00 – 75.00 C. *Metz Superlatives Auction.*

Cards, plastic, "Drink
Coca-Cola," lady with
dog in unopened
package, 1943, M,
$235.00 – 250.00 C.

Cards, plastic, "Drink
Coca-Cola," military
nurse in uniform with a
bottle of Coke, 1943, M,
$145.00 – 185.00 C.
Mitchell Collection.

Cards, plastic,
"Drink Coca-Cola,"
wartime spotter
lady, 1943, M,
$125.00 – 145.00 C.
Mitchell Collection.

Cards, plastic, "Drink Coca-Cola,"
stained glass look, in original
unopened package, 1974, M,
$15.00 – 20.00 C.

Cards, plastic, "...It's the Real
Thing," bottle and food, in
original unopened package,
1974, M, $25.00 – 30.00 C.

Cards, plastic, "Have a Coke and a
Smile...Coke Adds Life," unopened
double deck, 1979, M,
$40.00 – 50.00 C.

Cards, plastic, Sprite Boy with bottle cap hat and bottle of Coke, in unopened package, 1979, M, $45.00 – 60.00 C.

Checkers, wood and metal, "Coca-Cola" with dynamic wave logo on board, modern version with metal pegs for the actual checker pieces, 1970s, EX, $65.00 – 85.00 C. *Mitchell Collection.*

Checkers, wood, "Coca-Cola" in script on top of each checker, in original cardboard box that is marked "Compliments of the Coca-Cola Bottling Company," 1940 – 1950s, EX, $45.00 – 75.00 C. *Mitchell Collection.*

Dominos, wood, "Compliments of the Coca-Cola Bottling Company," in original cardboard box, 1940 – 1950s, EX, $65.00 – 95.00 C. *Mitchell Collection.*

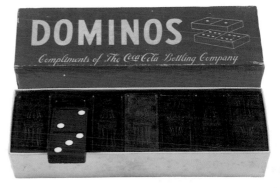

Puzzle, cardboard, "Drink Coca-Cola 5¢," Victorian lady with a glass of Coke in a glass holder, 500 pieces, VG, $75.00 – 95.00 C.

Puzzle, cardboard, "Coca-Cola," featuring various poster scenes, completed and mounted on wall board, VG, $100.00 – 115.00 C.

Puzzle, cardboard, "Drink Coca-Cola Ice Cold," 1,000 pieces in original box with scene of young lovers on a Coke cooler in front of an old country store, EX, $25.00 – 45.00 C. *Metz Superlatives Auction.*

Bandana, cloth, "Kit Carson" and "Drink Coca-Cola," red with Kit in center and western scenes plus Coke logos in each corner, 1950s, 20" x 22", EX, $75.00 – 125.00 C. *Mitchell Collection.*

Belt, web, "Enjoy Coca-Cola" on metal buckle with dynamic wave logo, 1960s, NM, $20.00 – 30.00 C.

Belt, web, "Enjoy Coca-Cola" on metal buckle with white and red dynamic wave logo, EX, $20.00 – 30.00 C.

Coat, cloth, "Enjoy Coca-Cola...Central States Bottling Co.," green waist-length driver's jacket with zip-in quilted lining for light or heavy weather use, EX, $45.00 – 65.00 C.

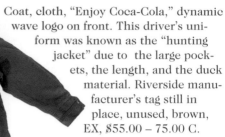

Coat, cloth, "Enjoy Coca-Cola," dynamic wave logo on front. This driver's uniform was known as the "hunting jacket" due to the large pockets, the length, and the duck material. Riverside manufacturer's tag still in place, unused, brown, EX, $55.00 – 75.00 C. *Metz Superlatives Auction.*

Hat, cloth, "Drink Coca-Cola," round logo on side of folding soda fountain attendant-type hat, NM, $55.00 B – 125.00 C. *Autopia Advertising Auctions.*

Hat, cloth, "Drink Coca-Cola," round logo patch on folding driver's cap, 1950s, VG, $70.00 – 100.00 C. *Mitchell Collection.*

Coveralls, cloth, "Drink Coca-Cola" round patch on front, 38R, VG, $125.00 – 145.00 C.

Patch, cloth, "Enjoy Coca-Cola," round jacket patch, 1950 – 1960s, EX, $20.00 – 40.00 C. *Mitchell Collection.*

Shirt, cloth, "Drink Coca-Cola," round patch on back of striped driver's shirt, VG, $45.00 – 55.00 C. *Mitchell Collection.*

Tie, cloth, "Enjoy Coca-Cola," with dynamic wave in red box on brown background, EX, $15.00 – 20.00 C.

Shirt, cloth, "Things Go Better with Coke," bowler's shirt with lettering on back, 1960s, EX, $30.00 – 45.00 C. *Mitchell Collection.*

Uniform pants and shirt, "Enjoy Coca-Cola," driver's set with dynamic wave cloth patch, white shirt with green pants, EX, $55.00 – 75.00 C.

Uniform pants and shirt, cloth, "Enjoy Coca-Cola," driver's issue by Riverside, still in original packaging, dynamic wave cloth patch, NM, $65.00 – 95.00 C.

Vest, cloth, "Enjoy Coca-Cola" cloth patch on chest, green, issued to drivers, EX, $35.00 – 55.00 C.

Vest, cloth, "Drink Coca-Cola" round cloth patch on front of driver's uniform vest, large "Drink" patch on back, elastic waist, EX, $70.00 – 100.00 C.

Vest, cloth, "Enjoy Coca-Cola," insulated uniform item with dynamic wave cloth patch over front pocket, this style seems to be the most popular with collectors, red, EX, $35.00 – 55.00 C.

Ad, paper, "...And Now the Gift for Thirst...Drink Coca-Cola," Santa with Coke and kids with gifts, 1952, 7" x 10", VG, $8.00 – 10.00 C. *B. J. Summers.*

Ad, paper, "And the Same to You," Santa in armchair with bottle of Coke, *National Geographic*, 1939, 7" x 10", VG, $8.00 – 12.00 C. *B. J. Summers.*

Ad, paper, "Coca-Cola," Santa with Coke bottle in the middle of train setup and with helicopter, 1962, 7" x 10", VG, $8.00 – 10.00 C. *B. J. Summers.*

Ad, paper, "Coca-Cola," Santa with little boy at referigerator with bottle of Coke, 1959, 7" x 10", VG, $8.00 – 10.00 C. *B. J. Summers.*

Calendar, paper, "Me, Too!" full monthly sheets, former owner had recorded the temperatures on each day, 1954, VG, $150.00 B. *Metz Superlatives Auction.*

Bottle hanger, paper, " 'Twas the Night Before Christmas,' " 1950s, M, $25.00 – 45.00 C. *Mitchell Collection.*

Display, cardboard, "Drink Coca-Cola Festive Holidays," in die-cut 3-D rocketship, 1950s, 33" tall, VG, $325.00 – 375.00 C. *Mitchell Collection.*

Display, cardboard, "Coca-Cola," die-cut easel back that folds out to 3-D effect with little boy in pj's surprising Santa, 1950s, VG, $235.00 – 275.00 C. *Mitchell Collection.*

Display, cardboard, "Greetings for Coca-Cola," die-cut standup with a Coke, 1948, 5' tall, F, $240.00 – 275.00 C. *Mitchell Collection.*

Figurine, porcelain, animated Santa holding the book with the lists of good and bad children, EX, $120.00 – 145.00 C. *Mitchell Collection.*

Figurine, porcelain, Royal Orleans, Santa beside fireplace, 1980s, EX, $135.00 – 150.00 C. *Mitchell Collection.*

Figurine, porcelain, Royal Orleans, Santa with a globe and bottle of Coke, complete set contains six figures, 1980s, EX, $200.00 – 225.00 C. *Mitchell Collection.*

Poster, cardboard, "Coca-Cola...Christmas Greetings," Santa with bottle of Coke and note left for him by child, 1932, NM, $4,200.00 B. *Metz Superlatives Auction.*

Figurine, porcelain, Royal Orleans, Santa and boy with dog, 1980s, EX, $140.00 – 155.00 C. *Mitchell Collection.*

Sign, cardboard, "Add Zest to the Season," string hanger with Santa and a bottle of Coke, Canadian, 1949, 10½" x 18½", EX, $900.00 B. *Metz Superlatives Auction.*

Sign, cardboard, wreath with Santa inside the circle, 1958, EX, $50.00 – 65.00 C. *Mitchell Collection.*

Sign, paper, "Santa's Helpers," truck-sized advertisement with Santa holding six bottles of Coke, 1960s, 66" x 32", G, $125.00 B – 195.00 C. *Metz Superlatives Auction.*

Ad, paper, "Come in...Thirst Knows No Season...Refreshment...Real Refreshment...Awaits" with Sprite Boy at soda fountain and wearing the soad fountain hat instead of the bottle cap, 1949, VG, $30.00 – 40.00 C.

Ad, paper, "Host of the Highway," vending machine and Sprite Boy on *National Geographic*, 1950, 6⅞" x 10", G, $8.00 – 15.00 C.

Ad, paper, "Where There's Coca-Cola There's Hospitality," with Santa looking in refrigerator, 1948, EX, $40.00 C.

Coaster, paper, "Have a Coke," 1950s, M, $12.00 – 15.00 C. *Mitchell Collection.*

Fan, cardboard, "Have a Coke," from the Memphis, TN, bottler, 1951, F, $65.00 – 80.00 C. *Mitchell Collection.*

Sign, cardboard, Coca-Cola six-pack with Sprite Boy in bottle cap hat, 1946, 41½" x 27½", EX, $525.00 B. *Metz Superlatives Auction.*

Sign, cardboard, "Coca-Cola...Take Some Home," Sprite Boy case insert, 1944, 10" x 13", NM, $220.00 B – 295.00 C. *Metz Superlatives Auction.*

Sign, cardboard, "Now! Family Size Too!" in original wood frame, 1955, 36" x 20", EX, $550.00 B. *Metz Superlatives Auction.*

Sign, Masonite, "Beverage Department," featuring a "Drink..." button in center of wings that have Sprite Boy on each end, Kay Displays, 1940s, 78" x 12", EX, $850.00 B – 1,000.00 C. *Metz Superlatives Auction.*

Sign, Masonite, "Drink Coca-Cola," arrow through chest-type cooler, 1940s, EX, $850.00 – 1,000.00 C. *Mitchell Collection.*

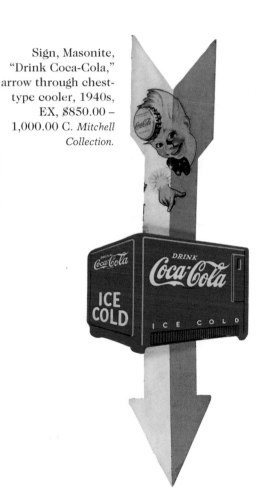

Sign, metal, "Have a Coke...Take Some Home," designed for bottle rack use, 1940 – 1950s, 16" x 23", EX, $300.00 B. *Metz Superlatives Auction.*

Sign, paper, "Come In...We Have Coca-Cola...5¢," line of marching glasses and Sprite Boy, 1944, 25" x 8", VG, $350.00 B. *Metz Superlatives Auction.*

Sign, paper, "Take Some Home Today...6 Bottles 25¢," window sign, NOS, 1950s, 25" x 10", NM, $300.00 B. *Autopia Advertising Auctions.*

Sign, porcelain, "Buvez Coca-Cola...Glace," French, 1954, 17½" x 54", EX, $235.00 C.

Countertop, metal, "Drink Coca-Cola...Ice Cold." Bolt-on type with single spigot, this style is sometimes referred to as the "outboard motor" due to the resemblance. 1940 – 1950s, VG, $750.00 – 825.00 C. *Patrick's Collectibles.*

Countertop, metal, "Drink Coca-Cola," single spigot with lift top by Dole, 14½" x 11½" x 25", G, $675.00 B. *Metz Superlatives Auction.*

Countertop, metal and plastic, "Drink Coca-Cola" painted on side, salesman's sample with fabric zippered carrying case, three heads, 1960s, EX, $975.00 C.

Play toy, plastic, in shape of single-spout dispenser, "Drink Coca-Cola," 1950s, EX, $175.00 – 210.00 C. *Mitchell Collection.*

Stadium, plastic and metal, "Carry Pack...Drink Coca-Cola," plastic outer housing with a two gallon tank and the original cup dispenser on the side, 1940s, EX, $800.00 B. *Metz Superlatives Auction.*

Bench, wooden, "Drink Coca-Cola..."
The rest is somewhat obscured, but
probably says "In Bottles," 1940 – 1950s,
F, $850.00 B.

Camera, plastic, "Coke Adds Life to Happy
Times," Polaroid camera, EX, $75.00 –
125.00 C.

Book mark, paper, "Drink
Coca-Cola 5¢," 2" x 6",
EX, $400.00 – 475.00 C.

Card table, metal and composition, advertising in each corner for Coke and advertising sheet on underside that boasts the table is so strong it will hold the weight of a grown man, 1930s, VG, $275.00 – 325.00 C.

Desk set, plastic, "Drink Coca-Cola," pen and music box, cooler shaped, 1950s, EX, $275.00 – 295.00 C.

Flower hanger, wall hung, metal, glass and wire, "Drink Coca-Cola," 1950s, EX, $450.00 B.

Key tag, composition, "Coca-Cola Bottling Co.," postage guaranteed, VG, $40.00 – 50.00 C.

Milage meter, metal, "Drink Coca-Cola...in Bottles...Travel Refreshed," 1950s, EX, $1,550.00 B.

Needle case, paper, Coca-Cola calendar girl with both a glass and bottle of Coke, 1920s, EX, $65.00 – 95.00 C.

Statue, composition, "Tell Me Your Profit Story, Please," man holding bottles of Coke, used as a selling training tool, 1930 – 1940s, EX, $175.00 – 195.00 C.

Straws, cardboard box, "Delicious and Refreshing," Coke bottle on all sides, 1930s, VG, $400.00 B.

Straws, cardboard box, "Have a Coke," Coke cup on each side, 1960s, EX, $225.00 C.

Tape, vinyl, "Coke Adds Life To..." reel-to-reel tape with 16 advertising spots for radio play, in original cardboard sleeve, 1970s, EX, $25.00 – 35.00 C.

Umbrella, canvas, "Drink Coca-Cola in Bottles" with bottle image, 1932, VG, $550.00 B.

Umbrella, canvas, "Drink Coca-Cola...the Pause That Refreshes," designed for beach use, 1930s, G, $110.00 B.

Umbrella, fabric, "Drink Coca-Cola...Be Really Refreshed," F, $500.00 – 600.00 C.

Wall pocket, fiberboard, "Drink Coca-Cola," 9" x 13", EX, $650.00 – 800.00 C.

PAST TYME PLEASURES

Purveyors
of
Fine Antiques & Collectibles
Presents Annual
Spring and Fall Antique Advertising Auctions

Call, fax, or e-mail today to be added to our
mailing list to receive future auction information.

*To receive the next color catalog
and prices realized, send your check for $15.00 today to:*

PAST TYME PLEASURES
PMB #204-2491 San Ramon Valley Blvd., #1 • San Ramon, CA 94583

PHONE: 925-484-6442, 925-484-4488 / FAX: 925-484-2551
CA Bond 158337

e-mail: pasttyme1@comcast.net   website: www.pasttyme1.com

Sales include many items with a fine selection of rare signs, trays, tins
and advertising items relating to tobacco, sporting collectibles,
breweriana, soda, talc, general store, etc.

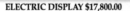